Nancy!
Enjoy the book
and your journey!

Patti Ward

Sit Back
and
Enjoy the Ride

Enjoying the Trip to Heaven

Patti Womack

WESTBOW
P R E S S®
A DIVISION OF THOMAS NELSON
& ZONDERVAN

Scripture taken from the New King James Version. Copyright © 1979, 1980,
1982 by Thomas Nelson, Inc. Used by permission. All rights reserved.

WestBow Press books may be ordered through booksellers or by contacting:

WestBow Press
A Division of Thomas Nelson & Zondervan
1663 Liberty Drive
Bloomington, IN 47403
www.westbowpress.com
1 (866) 928-1240

Because of the dynamic nature of the Internet, any web addresses or
links contained in this book may have changed since publication and
may no longer be valid. The views expressed in this work are solely those
of the author and do not necessarily reflect the views of the publisher,
and the publisher hereby disclaims any responsibility for them.

Any people depicted in stock imagery provided by Thinkstock are
models, and such images are being used for illustrative purposes only.
Certain stock imagery © Thinkstock.

ISBN: 978-1-5127-1924-6 (sc)
ISBN: 978-1-5127-1925-3 (hc)
ISBN: 978-1-5127-1923-9 (e)

Library of Congress Control Number: 2015918558

Print information available on the last page.

WestBow Press rev. date: 11/06/2015

Dedication

This book was birthed out of devotional e-mails I sent to a friend who also works in education. I sent one devotional daily to help jump-start our day at school. She kept telling me I should write a book. So, Marcy Winter, this book is dedicated to you, my friend. Thank you for giving me the push it took for me to step out and share what I love to do. I'm thankful God allowed our paths to cross so we could help each other on our journey to heaven. You've made the ride enjoyable.

Preface

I'm very directionally challenged. I can get turned around and end up getting lost leaving a parking lot. Please tell me to turn right or left, not north or south. Thank goodness for that little compass in my car's rearview mirror. That lady inside my phone's GPS even gets testy when I can't seem to follow her directions. She is always recalculating. I then find myself taking yet another lap around the block to get back on the right road. Today there isn't really any excuse to get lost with all the technology that lets us know our location at all times. We just need to avail ourselves of this great convenience.

The same is true spiritually; there's no excuse for losing our way with all the books, the Bible, and the Holy Spirit to lead us and keep us on the right track. This book is just a collection of devotionals out of my heart about different situations I've encountered on my journey. They are in no certain order or in a time frame. Just enjoy reading it at your leisure. Hopefully this little book will give you encouragement and direction as you travel to heaven. Nothing is better than a road trip, especially if you go with a friend and know where you're going. So let's enjoy our trip to heaven together and delight in reading about what we can do when life happens to us.

Breathe or Blow a Gasket

I sometimes become tired of people who continually have a negative attitude. No matter how many times you try to steer them down a more positive path, they soon veer off again. What's ironic about this situation is that when I become frustrated with their attitudes, they end up giving *me* an attitude.

We need to guard against this tendency to become negative when we feel our emotions or attitudes heading south. I had a heating-and-air guy preach a sermonette to me one evening and didn't realize that was what his service call had become, although I must say that he did take up an offering when he charged me for his services. He said that as long as there are moving parts, they don't last forever, and they certainly have more of a chance to continue working if they are maintained. Obviously he didn't think, by the looks of my furnace unit and its filter, that I had that done very often, if at all. He was right, of course.

Yes, my heating and cooling units will get dusty, and everything else will clog up my vents, my drains, and whatever else is involved with the moving parts. In the same way, spiritual life will get stifled, lose its effectiveness, and become stagnant because of attitudes, feelings that are stuffed down, or problems that make us want to blow a gasket. We maintain our spiritual moving parts by giving them to God and letting Him help with whatever is bugging the ever-loving delights out of us.

Philippians 4:4 says, "Rejoice in the Lord always. Again I will say, rejoice!"

Attention Grabber

Hey! What gets your attention? This varies with different personalities. With some people, it takes just a touch or look to get their undivided attention. Others may need more of a jolt to get them to focus on what's going on. Then there are others who are simply oblivious and don't even know what's going on around them.

Being a teacher, I have seen all of the above in my classroom. Sometimes we get so caught up in doing the game plan and getting it right, organized, or funded that we sometimes forget to look to our Coach for strength, direction, or just encouragement. Then we get discouraged when the plan isn't working, the money isn't covering the need, or people are just being people; then come frustration, irritation, and stress.

We need to stop, look over toward third base, and get our Coach's sign to proceed with our game plan. Because just like a coach, God will get our attention one way or another. One night while lying on the couch, I felt the floor shake and realized we were experiencing an earthquake in Wichita, Kansas. I can tell you that God had my full attention. It shouldn't take a jarring like that to get our attention or remind us of a truth. When we spend time with the Coach, all it takes is a check of the Spirit, a little prick of our conscience, or just a gut feeling of discernment. All these come through the Word and time spent in prayer. So let's be in a place where we can hear the still, small voice and not be so consumed with obligations of life that God has to shout to be heard above all the distractions that can cover up His voice.

Colossians 3:2 says, "Set your mind on things above, not on things on the earth."

Apple of God's Eye

In chapter 1 in Deuteronomy Moses turned over the leadership to Joshua and was soon going to die. He reminded the people of Israel of all God had done on their behalf and said that though they had been through many tough situations, God really loved them. Moses made a statement in this chapter that is an encouraging thought for us today. We're the apple of God's eye. Some of us here on earth are, or were, the apple of our dad's eye, but how awesome is it to know that we're the apple of the eye of the God of the universe?

Just like He did for the Israelites, He knows where we are in our wilderness. He will instruct us on how to maneuver through that wilderness, and He will always surround us with His protection. So mark it down, my fellow Christian; we're pretty special to God. My dad always carried my senior picture in his billfold; I like to think that if God had a wallet, my picture would be in there as well.

Deuteronomy 32:10 says, "He found them in a desert land, and in the wasteland, a howling wilderness. He encircled, He instructed them, and He kept them as the apple of His eye."

Afraid of the Dark

I can't say I've been afraid of the dark, but I haven't been a real fan of it either. I know one thing for sure: I don't like *staying* in the dark.

Spiritually we run into dark places. Some of these places can be doubts, fears, worries, sicknesses, circumstances, or disappointments. These are just a few on a long list. We might be in the dark, waiting to receive our answer to a prayer, to be healed, to feel confident in our faith, or to have the courage to step out of our comfort zone and be completely at rest in God's will and direction for our lives. We need to step into the light; then things will look differently to us than from our viewpoint from the shadows.

Spiritually if there is light, then there is Jesus. If there is Jesus, then there is a firm belief for any doubt, courage to replace the spirit of fear, trust to cancel out our worry, healing for the body and mind, victory over any trying circumstance, and joy in our sorrow. Physically our bodies will adjust to the darkness, and we can manage to see a little bit and move about somewhat. But spiritually we don't need to get used to dark places. We can practice walking in the light to dispel any darkness the Enemy may cast across our path today.

First John 1:5 says, "This is the message which we have heard from Him and declare to you, that God is light and in Him is no darkness at all."

What Attitude Are You Toting Around?

We have always taught kids to have a good attitude. We say to them, "You need an attitude adjustment." But then as adults we show rotten attitudes about many things and just call it like it is. We can't be sure of what we will encounter each day, but we can determine beforehand what kind of attitude we will have about whatever we do encounter. Some people borrow trouble from tomorrow and already have an attitude of negativity before they even get to the problem or before they even get to the bridge; they start crossing it with a bad attitude.

Sometimes we need to be reminded of what a good attitude looks like. One tip would be to be on the side that is positive. Some think people who are positive live in a fantasy world, because after all, life stinks at times. That is true, but that doesn't mean we need to stink along with it. We need to see what we can do that will add to the solution, not the problem; we need to see what we can do to make the situation better, not worse. No matter how dark things become, we should always try looking for the light at the end of the tunnel and help others find that light as well. The difference between having a good or bad day, going forward or moving backward, or having an effective witness or marring the cause of Christ depends on our choice of attitude for that day, that situation, or just that moment.

John 15:11 says, "These things I have spoken to you that My joy remain in you, and that your joy may be full."

Appraisal Is Good for the Soul

Sometimes we need to take inventory of how well we're growing and maturing in Christ. Just because we may have been saved for a long time doesn't necessarily mean we're spiritually maturing. We could ask ourselves some questions to see how we're doing. One question could be, are we really happy, genuinely challenged, and fulfilled? We might not even equate being fulfilled as spiritual or being a way to see whether we're growing up in Christ. The Word talks about being content, so if we can get that down, we can certainly be happy. We might not think that what we do as a job keeps us challenged, but if we're looking for opportunities to help to make someone's life easier and show the love of Christ, then that can keep us on our toes; and then we're challenged.

The question about fulfillment can be answered in that we can always think of a better situation to be in, whether it's finding a better-paying job or sharing our life with someone else. So if we don't have these desires met, can we be fulfilled? The Word speaks about a relationship with Christ being all we need on this side of heaven. So yes, we can be happy, challenged, and fulfilled with whatever hand is dealt to us. The Word also says we're made strong in our infirmities. So we grow in the fire, in the tough times, and when we encounter resistance.

I used to have a membership at the YMCA. I worked out on machines that created resistance for my muscles. One day I noticed a difference in my body. The same applies spiritually. Did I master every exercise machine at the Y? No, and I haven't mastered everything that has come my way to grow spiritually. But I can see day by day that God is faithful, and I can see spiritual growth. Not only can we see it with ourselves, but others will notice the growth as well.

Psalm 139:23–24 says, "Search me, O God and know my heart. Try me and know my anxieties. And see if there is any wicked way in me. And lead me in the way everlasting."

Blind Spots

How many times have you been driving along and decided to change lanes, check your mirror, and start to move into the lane—only to jerk the steering wheel back before you ran into a car that came out of nowhere? That car was in your blind spot. You would think you could see something that was right beside you.

The same experience happens to us in other contexts as well. We all have blind spots with ourselves and our kinfolk. Little Johnny's mom doesn't see that he isn't such an angel, or we don't see that we're at fault at times. This is good when we have our family's back, but we need to see that we all have blind spots we need to address every once in a while. The Spirit can reveal blind spots to us, and He is the best One to do it. Someone close to us can also help reveal a blind spot to us by gently instructing us or giving us a heads-up of what damage is being done if we continue in our way.

The Word says that many times we see something small in others, while in fact we have a very big issue going on right beside us in our blind spot. The Word tells us to confess our faults one to another in James 5:16. Confession helps us to see our dependence on God and the family of God. Some people choose to ignore their blind spots, some people deny them, and some really don't care whether what they do hurts other people or themselves.

While driving, we can't just depend on that mirror to do our looking for us; we have to literally turn our heads and look at what is beside us before we run into someone else. This takes some effort on our part to keep from getting into a wreck. The same is true spiritually; we must make an effort to work on our blind spots or our faults so we can be more effective in our walk with Christ. It's easy to say, "That's just how I am. Deal with it." But Christ died to help us change how we are.

Matthew 7:3 says, "And why do you look at the speck in your brother's eye but do not consider the plank in your own eye?"

The Before and After Effect

Many advertisers give us the "before picture" and then the "after picture." We see the wrinkled face before the person used the cream and then the nice, smooth face after the person used the cream. We see the overweight body in the before picture, then the nice, trim figure in the after picture. We see the before picture of the gutted-out house, then the picture of the remodeled house.

That is how we are in the before Christ picture and then the after Christ picture. Lives are changed, and people are on a different path, having made a 180-degree turn in actions, speech, and reactions. I was privileged to hear someone's life story of recovery from substance abuse; it was a before Christ story, and now it has become an after Christ testimony. We all have a story. If we're new creatures in Christ, we all have a testimony. We tell people about what God has done in someone else's life, but if we've been changed, forgiven, and washed clean, we owe it to the One who died for us to tell others what He has done in our lives.

Second Corinthians 5:17 says, "Therefore if anyone is in Christ, he is a new creation; old things have passed away; behold all things have become new."

A Balancing Act

One day I found myself walking the tightrope of trying to stay balanced. I had failed miserably by not bringing harmony to most of the situations I encountered that day. The problem was walking in the flesh big time.

But life is all about balance. We balance our checkbooks (okay, some people do), we try to eat a balanced diet by eating some food from each food group and just the right amount, and we try to balance our day to fit everything in that needs to be done. Our bodies were created so we could walk in a state of equilibrium. If not, then we would all fall facedown in the dust when we got up to walk. Mentally we were created to be stable and balanced in our emotions. So when things become unbalanced, we run to the bank to take care of the overdraft. When the diet becomes unbalanced, we become sick or anemic. We run to the doctor to get us back on track, and when our emotions run wild, we find the right pill to counteract those feelings.

On the day I became spiritually unbalanced by walking in the flesh, I should have stopped and tried to see what I could do to counteract my bad attitude, moodiness, and not-so-Christ-like spirit. Because I chose to continue in the flesh, I had to do damage control. That included going back and apologizing for my unbalanced actions. We can blame circumstances, other people, and even the season of life we're walking in for our failure to stay on the tightrope of spiritual balance. If we're in a state of equilibrium bodily, mentally, or spiritually, we bring harmony to whatever situation we meet. So why do we choose to walk in the flesh and even stay there for a time? That's a good question. We can get up every day and stay on the tightrope of life by choosing to walk in the Spirit.

Galatians 5:16 says, "I say then: Walk in the Spirit, and you shall not fulfill the lust of the flesh."

Know When to Duck or Say No

We live such busy lives. Our calendars are full of activities and places where we need to be. We run ourselves ragged by trying to cram everything in so no one will be hurt if we don't make his or her event. We sometimes want to say no, but we see that no one else has stepped up to the plate to do something, so we say yes. But I think it's important to step back, put our priorities back in place, and know when to quit saying yes every time.

We may think ducking out of something is a coward's way of dealing with something, but I think it would do our spiritual well-being a favor to duck out of negative conversations or situations that would bring us down spiritually. Sometimes it's hard to know how long to stick to something we're involved with, especially if it seems to be hard, difficult, or discouraging. We weren't promised easy strength. We're instructed in God's Word to endure to the end. Endurance isn't something negative or hard; it means to gather strength and finish strong. When all is said and done, it isn't how we start our race but how we finish it that will count for eternity.

Ecclesiastes 9:11 says, "I returned and saw under the sun that the race is not to the swift, nor the battle to the strong."

What Blows Us Out of the Water

When we think about this title, we immediately go to something we believe we're strong in and say there's no way anything would blow us out of the water. But really, we need to go to our weaknesses first. Sometimes we see our strengths, not what we want to admit would spiritually kick our tails. But in all reality, we're weak within ourselves in every area of our lives. We have to see that only through Christ is Satan defeated in our life situations.

The Word says not to think of ourselves as strong, for that is when Satan will come in like a flood. When we know we're strong in different areas, we don't depend on the Holy Spirit for power; we tend to try to do things within ourselves, because we're comfortable doing so. But the Word warns us of what can happen with this behavior. In other words, we shouldn't get used to doing tasks on your own, because then we let our guards down, leaving ourselves wide open to the Enemy's attacks.

The good news is that we don't need to let Satan blow us out of the water. We need to always be mindful of the fact that we're but clay; we are dependent on Christ to ward off what the Enemy has planned to use to destroy us. I think we're going to be even more mindful of this fact in this day of great deceit, self-reliance, and the tendency of people to leave God out of the equation.

First Corinthians 10:12 says, "Therefore let him who thinks he stands take heed lest he fall."

Chains or Change

Someone once said to me that she thought Sunday was a sad day of the week. The reason was that when she was growing up, she wasn't allowed to do much on the Sabbath; hence she kept that mentality and never changed her feelings about the day.

Sunday is everything but sad for the forgiven, set-free child of the King. The Enemy had held her in bondage when Christ paid the price to set her free. Other chains of bondage for different people could be habits they can't break. Another mode of bondage is what other people think; thus this either hinders or hampers our freedom in Christ when we're around them. Intimidation is another way we can be bound and not experience full freedom. Fear, low self-esteem, lack of boldness to stand for the right, fear of failure, worrying about our future—those are just a few of the issues on a very long list. If the Enemy can use something to bind us so we don't experience freedom in Christ, then his battle is half won. So let's not allow something or someone to stifle the freedom we have in our relationship with Christ.

Galatians 5:1 says, "Stand fast therefore in the liberty by which Christ has made us free, and do not be entangled again with a yoke of bondage."

Feeling Blessed

When a Christian says he or she is blessed, this isn't because lives are free of trouble at the moment, because everyone is healthy, or even because all bills are paid. The reason we're blessed is because the Word tells us we're blessed with every spiritual blessing. In other words, when we receive Christ, we receive—or are blessed with—everything we need to get to heaven and enjoy the trip there. We can possess both physical and material blessings, but what a thought it is to know we possess spiritual blessings. God is all about our spirits more so than our physical capacities. Someone will bury our physical bodies, but our souls will live on.

We aren't blessed because of what we have or what we can see; we're blessed because of what isn't seen: a clear conscience, a pure heart, a forgiven soul, and eternal life. The rest is just temporary, just icing on the cake. We need to be grateful for all our blessings, both seen and unseen. Our culture teaches us that we're entitled to certain privileges, but we need to stop and be mindful of where our help comes from. We are guilty of taking many blessings for granted. So live gratefully today, because we never know what can happen in a day that will forever change our lives.

Ephesians 1:3 says, "Blessed be the God and Father of our Lord Jesus Christ, who has blessed us with every spiritual blessing in the heavenly places in Christ."

Pushing Our Buttons

The Scripture tells us to be happy when we face trials, because they make us stronger as Christians. Should we say, "All right. Bring it on"? No, we just need to learn how to react when trials come our way. The Enemy likes to stack up routine, everyday problems and overwhelm us until they grow into a regular crisis. So how do we react when our buttons are pushed?

When we look at those things that push our stressors, these will differ from one person to the next. What may make one person crazy may not even faze someone else. But we all need to decide for ourselves whether we're going to let something make us fly off the handle, or are we just going to let it go without letting it become an issue? The problems could be routine things throughout the day: maybe a grumpy boss or coworker, a disobedient child, burned toast, malfunctioning equipment, tardiness at work, or a flat tire. I'm just throwing out some examples of stressors that might punch our button for the day.

If we let everything pile up, irritations can turn into frustrations. Then something is said, and boom—we explode. In the explosion of emotions, we react unkindly, say things we later regret, and decide to stay in that mode and not try to stop the vicious cycle. Because of another stroll down the lane of the flesh, we affect not only our day but also the day of those who happen along our way. The Enemy loves it when we're held captive in the walk of the flesh, but happy are we when we decide ahead of time, or even smack dab in the middle of it all, to start behaving as a child of God and walking in the Spirit. This is a little like thumping a watermelon to see whether it's ripe. Sometimes we get thumped, and others soon find out by our reactions whether the fruit of the Spirit is ripe and ready in our lives.

James 1:2–3 says, "My brethren, count it all joy when you fall into various trials. Knowing that the testing of your faith produces patience."

I Would Give You a Kidney

We have all heard these expressions: "I would take a bullet for you" or "I would give you a kidney." When we say these things, we tell someone that he or she means a lot to us. We would do what it takes to make sure that person is safe and healthy. We've all seen in a movie or TV show when the hero throws himself in front of the bullet, saving whoever the target was in the first place. We've also read stories about people being the perfect match to save the life of someone on a kidney donor list.

We had a tornado drill at school, and the assistant principal became a spiritual visual aid when he showed us what the older kids do for the younger ones. He told the older kids to use their bodies to shield the smaller kids. Wow, what a visual of what Jesus does for us in our spiritual storms; He covers us. In the Word He told Jerusalem that if the Jewish people had just come to Him, He would have covered and protected them just like a hen would do for her chicks. The Word also tells us that He took the ultimate bullet for everyone when He died on the cross and took the death meant for us. Sometimes it's good to remember the sacrifice He made for us to have life.

Psalm 91:4 says, "He shall cover you with His feathers. And under His wings you shall take refuge."

Critical Spirits

When we're critical of others or anything, we allow a spirit of criticism to invade our beings. The key is discerning between giving constructive criticism and being downright critical. There's a big difference. The key is knowing how and when to criticize. We've all been on both sides: the one criticized or the one criticizing. We know it's easy to be critical and not to be constructive. We're quick to see what's negative or what will go wrong instead of focusing on what's positive, what has already been done, or what has already worked in the situation.

I read an article in which someone used a cell phone as an example. People fuss about how slow their cell phones are, how long they take to make a connection, or whether the phones keep them waiting for five seconds. Not once do they think of how awesome it is to be able to communicate with people thousands of miles away in just seconds. We don't usually communicate that type of gratitude about our phones, but let them drop a call or disconnect us, and boy, do we make it known that we own a piece of junk. Hence we see a critical spirit that sees only the flaws in situations or even in people. Sometimes we just need to be reminded of what is right in this world and not let what is wrong become our central focus. We never know what our words or actions will do to or for someone today. So we must use wisdom, and if we need to be critical, let's have a better way or solution to the problem. Otherwise it's just a negative put-down, not a positive edification of the person or situation.

Proverbs 9:10 says, "The fear of the Lord is the beginning of wisdom. And the knowledge of the Holy One is understanding."

Bellyaching

The children of Israel had a pesky problem God detested as much as their idolatry. That problem was called murmuring. Some synonyms of this word are bellyaching, griping, whining, complaining, and moaning. We've probably bellyached about a few issues in the last twenty-four hours or less. So really, we can't fault the Israelites in their vicious cycle of disobedience when we do the same thing. Or maybe we find comfort in the thought that even God's chosen people couldn't get it right. Either way, God wants us to fix the attitudes in our lives.

What's easier to do? Complain or compliment, bellyache or be grateful, gripe or grin, moan or move on? We already know the answer, so a good reminder to ourselves today would be to choose not to murmur. But here comes the day and its problems. People in our work space do stupid things, and we need to gripe about them. We don't feel 100 percent, so our thoughts tend to fall out of our heads via our mouths when really they should stay in our heads. There may even be things that happen that we actually have a legitimate beef about. But let's not let history repeat itself, and let's learn our lesson more quickly than the Israelites did. Let's be the ones who compliment, encourage, and build others up in our world. We need to crush the desire to gripe and just be positive or quiet. We decide what we do.

Philippians 2:14 says, "Do all things without complaining and disputing."

Comfortable in My Skin

When I had a membership at the YMCA, I saw a guy who was obviously comfortable in his skin. He wore Hawaiian flower shorts, a white T-shirt, and kneesocks as his workout outfit. That's not attire you'd find in the sporting wear aisle right now. But buddy, he was in shape. Being comfortable in one's skin can involve a lot more than just looking good. Society has put a high premium on being good looking. People set many different bars, and the bars are especially high for our youth. If we don't measure up, then we experience depression, intimidation, rebellion, or bitterness.

But we can be comfortable in our skin when we accept ourselves as we are. Should we strive to be in good shape? Yes, the Word teaches us to take care of our bodies; after all in first Corinthians 6:19 it tells us we're the temples of the Holy Spirit. Do we try to hurdle over the bars society sets? We should always do our best in whatever we do. God wants excellence, not mediocrity.

Should we measure our progress according to society's standards? No, that's why it's so important to get Scripture inside us. Because in the end of all things, God's Word will be the yardstick by which we will be judged. But even we adults can get caught up in what the culture teaches and forget who we are in Christ. We're forgiven, secure, significant, free, loved, healed, protected, and delivered—just to name a few of the benefits we can claim from the Word.

First Samuel 16:7 says, "But the Lord said to Samuel, 'Do not look at his appearance or at his physical stature, because I have refused him. For the Lord does not see as man sees. For man looks at the outward appearance, but the Lord looks at the heart.'"

Lesson Learned from a Piece of Chocolate

A student gave me a box of chocolates. As it sat on my desk, I thought of a spiritual lesson I learned by trying to decide which piece I wanted by using the diagram on the lid. I could have chosen a chocolate without using the diagram, but I might not have cared for what I got. Or I could have been pleasantly surprised.

We have no idea what a day might bring, but what we choose to do with what we get makes all the difference in the world. Although we may not know what tomorrow holds, we still have a good guide to help us with our tomorrows. We have God's Word and the choice to take what we've been handed and give it to God. When choosing a chocolate, I can take time to look at the box lid and find out what I'm getting; then I won't be surprised with what I pop into my mouth. Or I can just randomly choose one, be very disappointed, and spit it into the trash can.

We can choose to use what we have to help others, or we can be a hindrance to those around us. It could be that what life has given us isn't easy to swallow, but we can choose to let God take it and use it to help us grow spiritually. We can help others with their bad news, difficult circumstances, or maybe a challenging diagnosis, because we had the very same things cross our paths. Then again, we receive blessings and benefits in life that are great. We don't need to feel guilty, because life is good. We need to be grateful and not take it for granted. So the Word is so true when it says we will be the happiest when we're content with whatever chocolate piece comes up for us to taste. The situation can be bitter or sweet, but whether we're bitter or better is all up to us.

Philippians 4:11 says, "Not that I speak in regard to need, for I have learned in whatever state I am, to be content."

What Can Happen While Standing in Line

Someone has said that over a normal life span, we will spend five years standing in various lines. Just think of the tasks we could accomplish in five years, but we won't get them done because we'll be standing in line. Someone suggested that we give that time to God. How in the world do we do that?

First, think of what we do in line. We talk to those around us or read the headlines of the magazines on the rack. But mainly we fuss and fume about how long it'll take for us to get to the front of the line. The bottom line is that many thoughts go through our heads while we stand in line. Some of us voice our thoughts, although some aren't edited before they come out of our heads, while others are positive and encouraging to whoever seems to be holding up the line.

This discussion goes back to the fact that our responses start with a thought. Much of the time we're so busy; that we're running to get to the next appointment on our calendar for the day. The line could be a good time for God to have our partially undivided attention, while the line slows us down for a space of time. This is partial attention for some of us who are easily distracted with things around us; if we gave our thoughts to God while in line, think of what we could do that would make standing in line more positive and profitable. Let God speak to us through our thoughts.

I like to think that God uses our thoughts as His e-mail address. We must be careful because the Enemy uses the same means to deliver his messages too. Quieting our thoughts and turning them toward God take discipline.

So the next time you're stuck in line, waiting for a train, don't be in such a rush to find a way to make a U-turn and get around the experience. Try turning your thoughts to God. The next time you're waiting in line to buy groceries (obviously the person ahead of you can't count to ten for the express line of nine items or less), just give an encouraging word to the stressed-out mother behind you. Another situation that bothers most is pulling the number 103 when someone just called number 73. Just breathe and enjoy some quality time with your Maker. Then when you get up to the crabby lady at the desk, you can give a smile instead of the same negative disposition she's handing out. So let's go find a line.

Psalm 139:23 says, "Search me, O God, and know my heart. Try me and know my thoughts."

Communication Is an Art

Communication isn't just the spoken word. We speak all day long one way or another. We use our mouths, body language, and vocal tones to communicate. Speaking is just half the equation; listening is the other half. There are positive and negative results with any of those ways to communicate. Some negative ways could be sarcasm, an eye roll, a shrug of the shoulders, not making eye contact, not giving attention to the speaker, interrupting the speaker, multitasking while talking with someone, finishing sentences for the speaker, and using the wrong tone while answering the speaker.

Just as there are negative ways to communicate, there are positive ways to get your point across. These could be giving the speaker your undivided attention, not looking around the room while conversing, not texting or checking phones, and responding at appropriate points in the conversation. Bad listening habits lead to bad communication habits. Really, when we think about it, we all want to be heard and have someone's attention for a space of time while talking with him or her. That is the downside of e-mails and texts today. With all our technology and conveniences, we leave the most important (and usually the most effective) mode of communication out of the picture: face-to-face conversations. The most important step for us to take today might just be to put down our phones and look into the eyes of someone who just might need our full attention.

Psalm 141:3 says, "Set a guard, O Lord, over my mouth. Keep watch over the door of my lips."

Spiritually Stressed Out

Sometimes I think we can be so saturated with the Word but fail to give it away that we become overweight saints on the pew. But on the other side of that coin, we can give out to the point that we run on empty by doing our ministries, working for good causes, or just showing up and being at our post of duty. That might sound like blasphemy; after all, we're doing God's work. But sometimes it's easy to be so busy with working *for* God that we don't always spend as much time *with* God.

The Enemy uses this card for Christians he finds to be faithful, committed, and busy at their post of duty. They are his best targets to bring discouragement due to lack of help, stress with so much to do, and impatience with the rest of the couch potatoes. I think it's interesting that the warning signs of being overweight and running on empty are the same. So either way the Enemy can get the overindulgent saint and the overworked saint. We need to strike the right balance and find time to refuel, push the refresh button, and just spend time with God. In Him we can find the restoration and rest needed to be all we can be at our posts of duty.

Psalm 23:1–3 says, "The Lord is my shepherd I shall not want. He makes me to lie down in green pastures. He leads me beside the still waters. He restores my soul. He leads me in the paths of righteousness for His name's sake."

The Gospel Simply Put

When we read the Gospels, we find this phrase popping up throughout the text: "And Jesus spoke this parable." The parable was simple and clear, bringing out what was important and communicating to whatever group He happened to have bumped into that day. That sounds like a great way for us to communicate the gospel as well.

We sometimes make things more complicated and harder than they should be. We don't consider who we're communicating with; we just put everyone in the same box when there are many levels of understanding represented. Other times we just go on and on about things that aren't going to matter next week; we just try to prove our point and not communicate the gospel at all. Some may even be tempted to show their superiority over someone with their knowledge on a subject. They may miss the whole point of the reason to witness, and that is to get the essential or important point across, not go over someone's head while doing so.

Jesus knew how to get His audience's attention and keep it by dealing with what fit their lives. One day He might be talking with farmers and another day with teachers, so He didn't give the same parable to both groups. Today we need to communicate with purpose, clarity, and discernment. Sometimes Christ spoke without words and just set a great example. Sometimes our best witness of Christ living in us is by living it out before our world.

Matthew 28:19 says, "Go therefore and make disciples of all the nations, baptizing them in the name of the Father and of the Son and of the Holy Spirit."

We Can Have It All

Do you ever say, "If I were this" or "If I had that" or "If this would happen, then my life would be complete"? Or maybe you've said, "If I were married," "If the house were paid for," "If I had better retirement," or "If I had a better-paying job." We may not dwell on these issues all the time, but the bottom line is that if we've received Christ, we have it all. We have salvation, hope, heaven, and peace. The Word tells us we house the Godhead. In other words, if we have received the Holy Spirit, part of the Godhead, then we get everything God wanted for man in the first place before the fall of Adam. Looking at it from that perspective helps with what we think is important in being whole as a person on planet Earth. Therefore no one, including ourselves, can make us think we're lacking today.

Colossians 2:9–10 says, "For in Him dwells all the fullness of the Godhead bodily. And you are complete in Him, Who is the head of all principality and power."

A Clear Conscience

The Word tells us about a time when Paul was put on trial for his faith before Felix. Paul tried to convince Felix to accept Christ. This story is great because we can still use this verse in the Bible as an encouragement for us today. We can live with a clear conscience. That is really something to be able to say in this day and age when people have pretty much seared their consciences. How awesome it is to be able to drift off to sleep without any guilt, to lay our heads on pillows and know that if we weren't able to wake and see another sunrise, all would be well. It's also great when we have a clear conscience with man. We can look everyone in the eye and know we've done nothing to cause him or her to stumble.

Will every relationship with others be great? No, but we can live knowing that we've done everything in our power to fix any rifts in relationships. Then regardless of whether others respond, we can still look them in the eye, knowing we've done all we can to clear our consciences. Felix was never convinced of his need for Christ, no matter what Paul said; but Paul could still enjoy his faith in Christ. Not everyone in our lives will be convinced; some people won't be happy no matter what we do or say. But they don't have to suck the joy out of our walk with Christ. Paul had to move on, as we've had to do at times. But we can have a good day, knowing all is well with our souls.

Acts 24:16 says, "This being so, I myself always strive to have a conscience without offense toward God and men."

Choices Make or Break Us

Sometimes society thinks if you have a degree or talent, that's what defines you as a person. But let someone make a bad choice, and we tend not to remember his or her ability; now everything is about the choice. We just remember the consequences of that bad choice.

We're faced with choices every day. Some are insignificant, such as what we will wear for the day. More significant choices could be choosing to mess up a relationship by making some bad decisions. From the time our feet hit the floor in the morning until we take off our shoes at night, we've made many good or bad choices.

As a teacher I sometimes see only part of a picture with a child who regularly makes bad choices. Sometimes we may have already quit with that person in our minds. If the person is good with making bad grades, then let him or her go with that. But as the child's teacher, my job is to find a way for him or her to want to make good grades. I can choose to help or to hinder, to encourage or to discourage, to smile or to frown, to lead or to drag, to be a teacher or to be a spectator. I don't want only to have the ability to teach; I want to have the heart of a teacher. This attitude can be true for any vocation you wake up to every morning. Choose to make a difference wherever God has placed you on this earth.

Joshua 24:15 says, "And if it seems evil to you to serve the Lord, choose for yourselves this day whom you will serve ... But as for me and my house we will serve the Lord."

Get Out of the Boat

Getting out of our comfort zones and stepping into the unknown are very hard steps to take. Writing this book was one of those times of stepping out and seeing whether I really had what it took to write it. I was just like Peter before he could walk on water; just as he had to get out of the comfort and security of the boat, so we have to climb out of what is safe to us. The goals we have may not be walking on water, but we still have the same fears connected with them: failure, rejection, someone's expectations, or even expectations of ourselves. Peter had to make a choice no one else in the boat had made. Sometimes we have to do what we know is God's will, even if our family, friends, or even Christian brothers and sisters don't see it as important or worth the chance to jump in. Peter had to forget what made sense and jump in with abandonment.

We need to quit trying to analyze and figure out everything before we jump. Peter stepped out during the storm, not when the water was as smooth as glass. We have problems stepping out when life is going great, let alone when we're in the middle of a storm. When Peter started going under, he immediately knew where his help would come from. We also know that, but when we're going down, caving in, or not doing anything out of our comfort zone in the Christian life, that is because we've lost our focus point. We've taken our eyes off Christ and focused on our circumstances. As long as Peter kept his eyes on Jesus, he walked on water.

According to the Word, we can do the same. Anytime we do what would be impossible in our own strength is walking on the water for us. Here's just a side note, but if there had been more encouragement from Peter's buddies in the boat, I wonder whether the story's ending would have included the whole boat load of disciples becoming water walkers. So go ahead and encourage someone or just lead the way and walk on some water.

Matthew 14:29 says, "So He said, 'Come.' And when Peter had come down out of the boat, he walked on the water to go to Jesus."

Our Faces Will Tell on Us

With one look at a person's face, we can immediately know what mood he or she is in that day. We can tell whether someone has been crying or maybe doesn't feel very well. Bad moods, disappointments, discouragement, worry, happiness, and joy are all registered on our faces. The Word talks about how worship will change our countenances. Will it change our circumstances? Not always. Will worship make all the pain go away? Probably not. Then why do it? God wants us to reflect His goodness. Life happens, but at the end of the day, God is still good. So we can at least let that goodness show on our faces.

When we spend time in the presence of God, He will show up on our faces. Just think of the times when you may not do well physically, emotionally, or even spiritually. See how your face can change in a heartbeat when you're caught up in a time of worship. So yes, our faces will tell on us. But on the other hand, they can also tell others whether we have been with Jesus.

Second Corinthians 3:18 says, "But we all with unveiled face, beholding as in a mirror the glory of the Lord, are being transformed into the same image from glory to glory, just as by the Spirit of the Lord."

What Will Really Count

We have heard it said that some people are too heavenly minded to be any earthly good. In other words, the person's head is spiritually in the clouds but needs to come down to earth and deal with the real world. But sometimes we can be so earthly minded that we don't take much time to think of what will count for eternity. There's a fine line between what's important in the spiritual realm and what has to be done in the physical realm, including time spent making a living and doing things that will last for eternity.

How much time do we spend on trying to make a difference in someone's life or to satisfy our own wants? How much time do we invest in others and where they will spend eternity compared to doing what we want to do? Yes, we must live and make a living, but there also needs to be an urgency about the soul of man and our souls as well. We always need to be prepared to leave when it's our time. Better yet, we need to be prepared to go up when Christ takes us out of here.

Matthew 5:16 says, "Let your light so shine before men, that they may see your good works and glorify your Father in heaven."

A Good Report

I remembered one summer when my friend shared with me that doctors had found a mass after her mammogram. My heart sank. I thought, *Oh no. This can't be happening.* So as we always do when we've worried and stewed about something, we decided to cover the matter with prayer. I even remember praying, "If it's cancer, just give it to me instead." But the report came back clear, and they told her to come back in six months. Well, my faith started shaking again when other signs showed up, and I began worrying all over again. But my friend said, "You have prayed. Leave it with God." Wow, I was supposed to be encouraging her. She is still clear; I believe God healed her.

That story makes me think we can receive different kinds of healing. The devil will use whatever he can to cripple us physically, emotionally, or spiritually. In the Bible Job felt attacks in every area of his life. Yet God found him to be upright, blameless, and faithful. My friend told me that doctors said the mass was just a cyst, and that was all. I believe God used this situation and my friend to teach me to persevere in prayer for healing and to leave this matter in His hands.

Proverbs 15:30 says, "The light of the eyes rejoices the heart. And a good report makes the bones healthy."

Driving under the Influence

"Driving under the influence" are words you don't want to hear after an officer stops you because you're either drunk or high. "Under the influence" simply means something is in control, and it isn't you. Spiritually we need to live under the influence of the Holy Spirit. That means the Spirit has control of all our actions, motives, thoughts, and words. But sometimes we find it easier to let others or the flesh influence us. We react, speak, or reveal what we're full of. The drunk reveals he's full of alcohol. The drug addict acts out of what his system has been shot up with. The flesh-walking Christian reacts out of what he or she is full of, which is self. But the Spirit-filled Christian gives out what he or she is full of, which is Jesus. May we get a renewed dose of Jesus today along with our morning cup of java or whatever else jump-starts our day.

Romans 8:5–6 says, "For those who live according to the flesh set their minds on the things of the flesh, but those who live according to the Spirit, the things of the Spirit."

God Has Our Backs

I love it when someone defends me after someone else has cast a bad light on me. Those kinds of friends are hard to come by, but it's so neat when you have them in your corner. But the psalmist spoke of One who is our defender against a more powerful foe than just someone trying to make us look bad. Christ is our defense against Satan. Satan can throw up accusations, but Jesus will intercept them and defend us to our heavenly Father.

He is also referred to as the Rock. The rock along the water isn't going anywhere. The waves may slam into it, and waves may wash over it, but it remains. That Rock is there for us who tend to move about in the storm. But the best thing mentioned in this same Bible chapter is that He is our salvation. Since there wasn't a cotton-picking thing we could do to save ourselves, there was God, who gave His Son as the one and only life preserver. We just have to decide whether we're going to receive that life preserver or try rowing our own canoes. Since I stink at the canoe thing, I'm glad I've trusted Jesus as my life preserver. Just remember this pleasant thought, my friend. God has our backs, as always.

Psalm 62:6 says, "He only is my rock and my salvation. He is my defense. I shall not be moved."

In a Slump

Many times at a place in Missouri called Silver Dollar City, I have watched potters shape clay for a vase or seen glass blowers craft a beautiful glass product. I've even watched the blacksmith pound out some steel to make horseshoes. Sometimes God uses the same process to help reshape or redirect us. The blacksmith must heat up the iron and pound the daylights out of a piece of metal that has lost its shape. But when he is finished, the piece of metal is useful and does the job it was meant to do.

God must reshape His instruments or vessels every once in a while to get us to be useful again. Is that process fun? No, because our passion level is zero, our enthusiasm is nil, and our attitudes can quickly start going south during this time. We can experience a spiritual slump, dryness, or a feeling of running on empty. So just as the baseball batter is in a batting slump and needs to find the sweet spot again or just as the gas tank in a car needs to be refilled so the driver can continue down the road, so we Christians need to find our sweet spot again and seek to be filled instead of trying to go on with no spiritual fuel. I think it's neat when God lets us see something He has shown us before by bringing it to our attention again. Some signs of spiritual dryness would be complaining, being hypercritical, or letting discouragement come on board. We need to recognize these issues when they raise their ugly heads and nip them in the bud instead of letting them take over our beings. We can stay out of our spiritual slumps.

Jeremiah 18:6 says, "O house of Israel, can I not do with you as this potter? Says the Lord. Look, as the clay is in the potter's hand, so are you in My hand, O house of Israel!"

Working against or through Struggles

Discouragement is a very good way for the Enemy to defeat us. He even uses it to trip up the very seasoned soul. It can come in the form of tragedy, sickness, stress, or weariness. Weariness could mean being physically or mentally fatigued. One would think the word *struggle* is negative, but one definition is "to contend with an adversary." That's exactly what discouragement is; it's an adversary. So the secret would be to struggle through and not struggle against and end up losing the war.

We need to form a habit of fighting to get through discouragement and not staying in that condition, because the longer we camp out there, the more damage is done. When we develop a habit of working through what discourages us, then discouraging us the next time is more difficult. Sometimes we just need to tell ourselves to suck it up and move on. We can't allow others to drag us along in their discouragement. We may be sad for a space of time, but we can't afford to wallow in self-pity. Throw a pity party but remember that parties come to an end.

Isaiah 41:10 says, "Fear not, for I am with you. Be not dismayed, for I am your God, I will strengthen you, yes I will help you. I will uphold you with My righteous right hand."

What Defines You

What tells others what is important in our lives? We print it on T-shirts, we buy bumper stickers proclaiming what it is, we tweet it on Twitter, we post it on Facebook, and now we can even wear it around our necks inside a life story locket. But what really tells others what is important in our lives is what we talk about, who we spend the most time with, and what we put the most money into. I purchased a life locket, and the charms I chose were an apple for my occupation as a teacher; a purple amethyst, my birthstone; a football for my love of watching college football; and a cup for my love of coffee. These charms may define me for things on planet Earth, but I have two others that are way more important than the other charms. Those charms are the word *faith* and a cross.

These two charms define me as a forgiven child of God, but in reality we give out our life story every day in one way or another. We need to show who and what is important in our lives by the example we send out with our lifestyles. The locket we wear around our necks is just backup for what we're living out. So yes, I'm a teacher. Yes, I love coffee. Yes, I was born in the great month of February; but the most important defining piece of my life is that I'm a born-again child of God.

First John 3:1 says, "Behold what manner of love the Father has bestowed on us, that we should be called children of God!"

Drama Free

We can live drama-free lives. When we think of drama, we tend to think of teenage girls. But just live long enough, and we can see that drama can slip into almost all age-groups. We can see it manifested in many places: on the job, in our homes, and even on Facebook. I can go on Facebook and see how some of my 735 friends have drama going on just by reading their posts or status updates.

But the good news is that we don't need to be sucked into relationships powered by drama. Those who always have to stir a pot of drama don't need to influence us. We can walk away from people who aren't happy unless something dramatic is continually going on in their lives. When there's drama involved, emotions are all over the place. It's healthy for us physically and good for us spiritually to walk drama free. We may not have problems with drama, which is good because there's no place for drama in a Christian's life. I used to teach drama, and it was needful for the student to be over-the-top emotional or dramatic. But in the classroom of life, check drama at the door and walk life with Spirit-controlled emotions.

Proverbs 29:11 says, "A fool vents all his feelings. But a wise man holds them back."

Delays

Delays can apply to something holding us up in a line at Walmart to wanting a situation in our lives to change when God seems in no hurry to change it. Delay also speaks of desiring something that hasn't come to pass yet. We must be reminded again that God's timetable isn't even close to ours, and what we have in mind may not even be what He knows is best for our lives.

So how do we accept this delay? Here are our choices: with a smile or sarcasm, with a blessing or a curse. Reactions and responses from a child of God are so very important to our testimony. Sometimes we want to blame our responses on medical issues, personality traits, and even other people. But instead of being hateful because of these issues, going ahead and taking the pill for the medical problem, we should ask Jesus to help with how we are and pray for those difficult people in our lives. Does God care about our small stuff? If it's big enough to affect our testimony, you bet He does. So let's go ahead and enjoy the trip, even when we're sitting in the waiting room.

Psalm 27:14 says, "Wait on the Lord; be of good courage. And He shall strengthen your heart. Wait I say on the Lord."

Slow Learners

We always seem to knock the children of Israel for going around the same mountain over and over again and not learning lessons. But we make the same mistakes in our lives. Just as the Israelites were on a journey, so are we. I always wondered why the children of Israel made the same mistakes over and over since they could literally see the presence of God in their midst via the cloud, the pillar of fire, and the bright light on the mountain. God told them what to do, and they did the opposite. God said He was going to give them the land of Canaan. He described the plan to a tee. They liked the sound of it but were afraid the inhabitants would take them captive, so they begged Moses to spy out the land. They didn't need spies, because God had already told them what was on the inside, and He would fight for them. But they sent spies, and the negative ones outnumbered the positive ones, so they started doubting all over again.

When I look back over my journey, I have seen the Lord work in my life and in the lives of others. Sure, I didn't have a cloud or pillar of fire, but I can't deny the presence of God I've felt. How many times do we do things in our own strength, knowing full well they won't work? How many times do we doubt, when our lives have been showered with God's guidance, His protection, and His blessings? How many times do we look at our circumstances and believe the negative report?

So we should give those Israelites some slack, because we can be like them in so many ways. They even had the ultimate GPS. I have to admit that I'm a wee bit directionally challenged. On a trip to Kansas City, I was heading to an address using a GPS. After I missed a turn, I found myself in a roundabout. I felt like an Israelite who had to take another lap around the mountain in the desert. I won't admit how many times I went around that roundabout, but I'm pretty sure the lady on the GPS was getting annoyed with me. I even found myself yelling at that invisible voice to let her know I wasn't happy with her directions, but she kept me in the roundabout anyway. I finally found my way out by listening to and not arguing with the GPS voice. Some things we don't want to hear, and some roads we don't want to travel, but God has a purpose. So instead of going in circles, let's learn our lesson so we can get on with the trip. There's no need to spend forty years in a wilderness, when the trip can happen in ten days.

Deuteronomy 8:2 says, "And you shall remember that the Lord your God led you all the way these forty years in the wilderness, to humble you and test you, to know what was in your heart, whether you would keep His commandments or not."

The Proof Is in the Pudding

We heard it as kids, and now we say it to kids: "Taste it. You'll like it." So children first smell the food; then they gingerly slip it into their mouths. Of course, two scenarios play out: they either spit the food back onto the plate with a disgusted look on their face or chew it up and swallow it with a smile. When the psalmist wrote about tasting to see whether God was good, he didn't try to convince a kid that some food was good, because the psalmist already knew God is good. He just reiterated the fact. The parent had tasted the food and knew it was delicious, so in turn he or she wanted the child to experience the same thing.

That's exactly what we as children of God need to get across to a world that needs to hear the message that God is good. We do that by being living proof that God is good by the evidence of the fruit of the Spirit modeled in our lives. Or we simply tell them like the psalmist did so long ago, taking the step of boldness and daring them to try it, knowing what the outcome will be. The parent had to experience the great taste of ice cream or some other delectable treat firsthand to be able to say with confidence to the child, "Taste it. You'll like it." So too we Christians must taste for ourselves and experience God firsthand to be able to share Him. So if God is evident in our lives, we obviously took the taste test and loved it. Who knows? This may be the very day someone needs what you've already experienced.

Psalm 34:8 says, "Oh taste and see that the Lord is good. Blessed is the man who trusts in Him!"

Just Claim It

One morning a friend of mine texted me this message: "It will be a great day. I'm claiming that!" I loved that. We as forgiven children of God hold the keys to the kingdom. The disciples and others in Jesus's ministry kept thinking the kingdom was going to be something set up on earth to overcome Roman rule. But Jesus tried to teach them, as well as us, that the kingdom wasn't a ruling factor to take over our enemy, but possessing the Holy Spirit within us enables us to bind on earth what is bound in heaven, and loose on earth what is loosed in heaven. We house the Holy Spirit, who gives us that power, if we allow Him to work through us. Then we can believe the promise of God and claim it as my friend referred to in her text that morning.

Do we have that privilege? Oh, yes. The Word tells us to knock, seek, and ask. It promises that if the door is opened, we will find and receive. Our problem is that when we pray, it's more like something we do instead of something we believe. How many times does answered prayer surprise us? The same response to answered prayed happened in the Bible when Peter's friends prayed that he would be released from prison; he showed up on the front porch, and they couldn't believe it was him. This is a prime example of just going through the motions of prayer but not believing God will answer it. So does that mean that if we claim it, we will always receive what we ask for? No, that would make God a "Santa Claus," but it does mean that we should allow the Spirit to have complete control of our actions, attitudes, motives, and reactions so we can move in that power. But prayer takes effort, time, practice, and discipline.

I know someone in Kansas who is a kingdom prayer warrior. She prays and believes as sure as the grass is green and the sky is blue. She has no room for doubt or an I-hope-so spirit when she prays about something. So does God have His favorites? No, but we need to consider how much the Holy Spirit is allowed to flow through our lives. When that happens, we don't need to design the answer, because we work with God's timetable, His set of circumstances, and His way. Some people get Jesus for a fire escape; others received Him and allow His spirit to flow through them so they can experience kingdom living here and now.

Matthew 16:19 says, "And I will give you the keys of the kingdom of heaven, and whatever you bind on earth will be bound in heaven, and whatever you loose on earth will be loosed in heaven."

Bosom Buddies

I have a saying on my wall at home that says: "Coffee tastes better with a friend." A close friend I refer to as my bosom buddy gave this picture to me. Coffee may not taste differently when you drink it with a friend, but I sure feel better when I can sit down with someone who is okay with me being myself and can tell it like it is. The bonus would be that the friend loves me and coffee.

A friend is a gift from God. Some friendships last just a little while and no more. Some experience a rough patch, and the friendship doesn't survive. But what a blessing it is to have a friend who knows the bad and the ugly as well as the good about you and still shows up and is there.

That's what Jesus does. He keeps showing up in our lives, even when we let communication deteriorate, when we keep messing up with what we know to do and aren't doing it. Jesus did the ultimate favor for friends; He died for us. In turn, we need to at least have patience with people who aren't on our Favorite List. Practice overlooking things, especially things that really won't matter in other people. I'm very thankful for all my friends, for the Word tells us that a friend comes alongside to strengthen us. So when a friend comes along and helps change or strengthen a friend's countenance, then we can accomplish what God designed when He thought of friendship.

Proverbs 27:17 says, "As iron sharpens iron, so a man sharpens the countenance of his friend."

Going through a Funk

"This too shall pass" isn't a Bible verse, but the words hold a lot of truth. When we go through a funk, there's always light at the end of the tunnel. We could go through a dry spell, but then we find ourselves in a church service where the Holy Spirit is moving. Or we may listen to some music on the iPod. God speaks through that speaker at church or through the song we happened to turn on.

The truth is, life is almost never as bad as it seems when our mood is low. We need to be like David in the Bible; he encouraged himself in the Lord. When we do this, regardless of the mood, situation, or emotion, the situation will truly soon pass.

I remember being in a low mood one day in the classroom. One of my fifth graders came up to my desk, and I read her shirt and had to smile. The shirt had these words on the front: "Take a chill pill!" God can use most anything to get His message across to His hardheaded children. So be ready to be used today to get someone out of his or her funk.

Psalm 124:1 says, "If it had not been the Lord who was on our side. Let Israel now say."

My Favorite Things

Here are some of my favorite things: coffee, Dr. Pepper, steak, road trips, a good book, a kindred spirit, golf, Oklahoma Sooner football, fried chicken, clean cars, a feel-good movie, having coffee with a friend, a comfortable outfit, pleasant surprises, finding a bargain, apple pie, porch swings, a day off, a good bubble bath, Southern gospel concerts, cool evenings, a nicely mowed green lawn, watermelon, the color blue, and Fridays. I'm just trying to have a more positive theme here. There is enough bad news, negativity, and complaining everywhere you look to last a lifetime.

So what do favorite things have to do with being spiritual? Not a thing, but they surely make a person feel much better when he or she thinks about something that makes him or her smile rather than what can get on his or her last nerve. The Word tells us exactly what we should think and meditate about to counteract the world's negative spirit. Go ahead and make a list of those things you love. See whether you don't end up having a smile on your face.

Philippians 4:8 says, "Finally brethren whatever things are true, whatever things are noble, whatever things are just, whatever things are pure, whatever things are lovely, whatever things are of good report, if there is any virtue and if there is anything praiseworthy-meditate on these things."

Friday the Thirteenth

We Christians don't believe in bad luck. Actually we don't believe in luck at all. But it's good to know that when a Friday lands on the thirteenth, we don't have to worry about what will happen as we go about our day. We won't worry about breaking a mirror, walking under a ladder (that's not superstitious—that's dangerous), stepping on a crack in the sidewalk, or doing anything else that may bring us "bad luck," according to the world. If we're in Christ, then we don't say, "As luck would have it" but "As God wills for us." And if we're children of God, we don't say, "The fates are against us" but "Life happens." We live lives that are blessed, not cursed. We are created by design, not by accident. We don't need to ask the eight ball what our future holds, because we know the One who holds our future. So the next time Friday the thirteenth comes up on the calendar, just call it another blessed Friday and walk with confidence in the One who has it all under control.

First Samuel 15:23 says, "For rebellion is as the sin of witchcraft, and stubbornness is as iniquity and idolatry."

Going Forward

I remember reading a story about a Georgia Tech player who picked up a fumble and ran it to the wrong end zone. One of his teammates tackled him right before he made a touchdown for the other team. Tech then punted, the ball was blocked, and the other team won by that safety, which cost Georgia Tech the game.

Life can be like that sometimes. We think we're doing what's right, even doing it with gusto, but we're going in the wrong direction. Sometimes it takes a good friend to gently turn us around, or sometimes we need something stronger to stop us abruptly and see that we're going in the wrong direction. The coach used wisdom and put the player back in the game. Jesus gives us that opportunity each time we mess up, make the wrong choice, or try to do it on our own.

How neat it is when a friend can help another friend in this game of life. How hard is it to see Christians working against each other? After all, we're all on the same team. I loved it when the coach made the decision not to bench the kid but to put him right back in the game. He didn't give the player a chance to feel sorry for himself or drag others down in his pit of despair.

We learn by living, and in that living we make mistakes or just plain sin. Blessed are the ones who learn from those mistakes and turn from those sins. We may learn from looking back into history, but we live from looking forward into our future. Encourage some soul today. You just might be the one who keeps that person from running to the wrong goal.

Luke 9:62 says, "But Jesus said to him, "No one having put his hand to the plow, and looking back, is fit for the kingdom of God.'"

Facebook Religion

One night I scrolled down my Facebook news feed and was amused by what people thought their seven hundred closest friends, including me, needed to know about them and what they were doing. Really, it isn't important that I know you're still in your pj's, you're on your way to the gym, you're having stomach issues, your child is teething, your sink is clogged, or that you looked out the window and didn't realize it was snowing, sleeting, or raining. I really don't need you to post pictures that are inappropriate. I don't need to know you have a foul mouth. I don't need to have to "listen" to you as you argue back and forth with someone else about religious beliefs. I just want to reach out to someone I can't, or haven't been able to, keep in touch with. I just want a post to encourage me down this road of life. I just want to share good things worth mentioning on a public platform.

We can remove ourselves from Facebook, but that isn't the only place where communication has gone bad. Our speech needs to be seasoned with love, our words chosen carefully, so we won't need to eat them or take them back. What comes out of our mouths should be something that brings life, not death. Just as we can remove ourselves from Facebook, we can remove ourselves from people who are consistently negative, who always tear others down or slander someone's name. Just as Facebook can be a great tool to help others down the road of life, so can words spoken to others help someone when he or she needs an edifying word. Words are powerful, but we need to use that power with care and prayer.

Proverbs 25:11 says, "A word fitly spoken is like apples of gold in setting of silver."

Faith

Sometimes it's hard to have faith about something because we let different things blind our eyes of faith. One could be flat unbelief. Another may not be unbelief but letting the Enemy cause others to place doubts in our heads. Others can do this by saying things that make us doubt ourselves, others, or God—all because we believe what we hear.

Another blinding factor is stressing about an unknown outcome. Could something go wrong? Yes. Does it sometimes go bad? Yes. When we're stressing, we allow Satan to distract us from going to our Helper. Sometimes we even go to our Helper but walk off with the problem instead of leaving it there. So if our faith is a little weak, think about what the reason could be and ask our Helper to help us see what He is able to do, not what circumstances tells us, what others say is true, or what our physical eyes see.

If you think about it, we experience faith every day. We have faith that chairs will hold us up every time we sit down. We have faith that the ton of metal traveling at seventy miles per hour won't cross the center line and hit us head on. We have faith that lights will come on when we flip switches. We have faith that our car motors will turn over when we turn keys in the ignitions. Our faith doesn't see what can go wrong; it expects cars to obey traffic laws, chairs to hold up weight, lights to come on, and cars to start, because that is what they are made to do.

God made us to be people of faith, but our eyes see what can and what does go wrong, and we expect that to be the outcome. Do cars wreck, lights go out, cars not start, or chairs collapse? Most definitely. But we first choose to believe they will do what they are made to do. So the lesson here is to always believe God will make the way, take us through the problem, defeat the enemy, and keep His promises.

Will the response be like we plan, how we plan, or when we plan? Not always. But our faith can't be shaken because of what our eyes see but because of what our God can and is able to do in our lives. We can rest in the fact that we have a giant-killing, sea-walking, death-defying, and miracle-working God. Keep the faith, fellow traveler.

Hebrews 11:1 says, "Now faith is the substance of things hoped for, the evidence of things not seen."

Grace

Think about what grace does for us, what kind of heart receives grace, and what the reaction to grace is when it's given. When we have experienced grace on our behalf, not by expecting it or thinking we deserved it but by humbling ourselves to the point that we see that God's grace is our only hope, then grace will make us see that our work ethics, morals, and obligations to others look a whole lot differently from the perspective of grace. Loving others will be second nature, gentleness will be evident in all our dealings with others, and serving God won't be something we do to get saved but *because* we're saved.

Last but certainly not least, we learn to overlook the faults of others and are quick to forgive their offenses against us. That is the picture of someone who has received and experienced grace. Yes, this analysis can be very convicting but not so condemning that we remember what we got in the bargain after we received His grace for our sins. So let's live grace-filled days and offer it to others on our way home.

Second Corinthians 12:9 says, "And He said to me, 'My grace is sufficient for you. For My strength is made perfect in weakness.'"

Throwing in the Towel

What makes us want to throw in the towel, give in, or just quit? We read in 2 Timothy that the author, Paul, sat in a cold, damp prison cell. He had no weight room, no televisions, no visits from family, and no free time out in the prison yard. He was chained, sick, tired, hungry, old, and imprisoned for his faith. Guess what he did? It's not what most of us would have done given the same circumstances. We would have been complaining, having the world's biggest pity party ever, and telling God what a rotten hand we'd been dealt.

Paul wrote to a young believer in Christ, encouraging him to fight the good fight, keep the faith, and follow the example of his teacher, mother, and grandmother. We find no whining of any kind in that book. We get all bent out of shape if someone doesn't speak to us, or we complain about the sermon going way too long or the musicians singing too loudly. In other words, it doesn't take much for us to complain or whine about our lot in life. We may not be imprisoned, but we may have to get out of our comfort zone to share or serve Christ.

Bottom line? Life isn't about us or our comfort. It's about how we can reach others and finish strong. So the next time we may feel like throwing in the towel, we should look around; there are people in our sphere of the world who count on us to stay in the ring and fight on.

Second Timothy 2:1, 3 says, "You, therefore my son, be strong in the grace that is in Christ Jesus. You therefore must endure hardship as a good soldier of Jesus Christ."

Guilt-Free Conscience

I love the thought that we can know and have a relationship with the God of the universe and that that same God, who spoke the world into existence, loves us. It's amazing to know that we can have our sins forgiven and to understand where we're headed after our eyes close in death. We can go to bed knowing all is well with our souls. It doesn't get much better than that. Then we can also throw in all the benefits and blessings of being a forgiven child of God. Sometimes we may think we have problems, but really, what can be better than no hangovers, no guilty conscience, no shame, and no chain from a habit that enslaves us and makes us powerless? When we choose Christ, that's the best move we could ever make.

Psalm 4:8 says, "I will both lie down in peace, and sleep. For You alone, O Lord, make me dwell in safety."

Use It or Lose It

In Second Timothy 1:6, Paul instructed Timothy to continue using the gift God had given to him. Paul talked to Timothy about keeping his faith. We can also take his words to mean our spiritual gifts too. Timothy and the church then fought the battle of not caving in spiritually due to persecution. We also fight the battle of maybe losing our passion, thus not using our gifts when given the opportunity. We may be good at something, but we're discouraged with the results or lack of them when we use our gifts. Paul told Timothy to stir or shake himself to get back a passion for the faith.

Sometimes we need to do the same thing with our gifts. "Use it or lose it" may not be altogether true, but when we're more concerned about results than about the perspective of eternity, we miss out on a blessing that someone else receives when we go ahead and use our gifts. So in whatever gift we possess, we need to use it with all our hearts, souls, and minds; then we need to leave the results in God's hands. Timothy had a cheering section with Paul, his mother, and grandmother, who helped him to stand firm. Let's encourage each other as the family of God to use our gifts, and really that's a gift in itself.

Second Timothy 1:6 says, "Therefore I remind you to stir up the gift of God which is in you through the laying on of my hands."

Gospel Hardened

Can we say we're gospel hardened? More than likely, we can say, "Yes, we are, especially if we've been raised in church, attended Sunday school, been to church every time the doors are open, signed up for Bible studies, or gone to Christian seminars." Some people let the Word go into them but don't apply the gospel to their walk with Christ. Others have heard the gospel so many times that they become too familiar with it and tune it out if they aren't paying close attention. Sometimes we've heard it so many times that we go ahead and finish what we think the preacher is trying to point out. We've already heard that sermon illustration before, so we don't tune in to hear whether God is speaking a new truth out of the same sermon.

To better illustrate my point, let me share another teacher story. One day before spring break, I continually said the same thing, including the phrase "Everyone needs to be quiet!" I looked around, and kids talked right after the words had left my mouth. I even asked this question: "Hey, class, what did I just tell you?" The class replied that I had told them to be quiet. I thought, *Then why aren't you doing it if you heard what I said?* They had become hardened to the same "gospel," because they had heard it so much that they tuned me out.

I then did something off the cuff. I announced to them they could go ahead and talk all they wanted. As soon as the words left my mouth, the class turned toward me with their mouths open. They weren't talking, but their mouths hung open in disbelief that I had just given them permission to talk to their hearts' content. I said, "Wow, you heard that loud and clear." I changed my method, and they heard me.

God may give the same gospel and use the same messenger, maybe even the same sermon illustration, but sometimes He wants us to sit up and listen when He decides to shake things up and bring out a new point for us to learn. After all, when we hear the Word taught, we listen to something that is so powerful, it will forever change people's lives.

Hebrews 4:12 says, "For the word of God is living and powerful, and sharper than any two-edged sword, piercing even to the division of soul and spirit, and of joints and marrow, and is a discerner of the thoughts and intents of the heart."

How Do We View Our Giants?

Someone could say that someone else looks like a giant to him or her. Of course this person could be three feet tall, and his or her giant could probably be five ten. So, from the perspective of looking up into this person's eyes, this is a giant. I thought about how we view our giants, and it's much like the example of a child looking up at an adult. Therefore, our effectiveness is blocked, and we freeze up when we think about or see our giant standing in front of us.

Giants can come in many different sizes, shapes, and personalities. Our giant could be a person, situation, or circumstance. We can't gauge the size of each individual's giant; we just know whether it's big enough to put fear in us. If it blocks or stifles us spiritually, then it has become our giant.

David didn't choose to go to battle with his ideas or man-offered options. He chose to believe God and stepped out with a sling, which he felt comfortable with. God had already seen him through other times of facing his giants. Sometimes we may think our "giant" won't ever go away or fall. David had more than one Goliath he had to face in his life. Overcoming it doesn't always happen with one blow, and it's over. Sometimes we need to do battle with our giants inch by inch. We always need to face our giants with a giant slayer point of view. Use what God provides for us to use and let Him do the rest. God has this one in the bag.

First Samuel 17:49 says, "Then David put his hand in his bag and took out a stone; and he slung it and struck the Philistine in his forehead, so that the stone sank into his forehead, and he fell on his face to the earth."

Spiritually Gullible

My friends sometimes have a heyday with my being a gullible person. My friend can mess with me and get me about every time. When we're gullible, we react without thinking something through and conclude that something that isn't true is true. Sometimes we can be deceived for a while, or we quickly catch on to the truth, but we can be caught again in no time. This can be funny when we're just messing with people to play tricks on them. I can laugh after I'm finished being upset with them for tricking me.

What would be tragic is being spiritually gullible or easily deceived so we turn the truth into a lie. It's so dangerous when someone can be so involved in sin that he or she is deceived into thinking all is well. Maybe the person becomes deceived into believing there is no hell, that God is all love and wouldn't send anyone there. All it takes to believe a lie is to listen to the wrong voices, spend time with the wrong people, and just twist Scripture to fit the present situation. Another way for someone to stay in a deceived state is for that person to constantly say something that isn't altogether true, then cover up for telling lies. The lies just keeps snowballing until that person wouldn't know truth if it walked up to him or her. In today's society of deceit, we must be on the offense and keep ourselves from being gullible with our never-dying souls. We need to guard our hearts so we aren't deceived. Don't believe everything you hear. Test it against Scripture; it's a safe place.

Romans 3:3–4 says, "For what if some did not believe? Will their unbelief make the faithfulness of God without effect? Certainly not! Indeed, let God be true but every man a liar."

What Grade Are We Making?

Every nine weeks during the school year, my job is to let parents know what grades their child is making. Along with grades, I have to fill out character strengths and weaknesses of each child.

One day I wondered what my card would look like as a Christian if someone were to fill one out for me. The first thing listed on the character traits is attitudes. Wow. How many times would we have an Unsatisfactory marked on the card because of some rotten attitudes thrown out there at times? Next on the list is obedience. As a teacher or parent, we desire kids to obey us, but how many times have we obeyed God grudgingly?

The next one is reaction to discipline. It isn't always comfortable to receive God's conviction or constructive criticism from one of His children, but what's needful for our walk is to suck it up and change what needs to be changed.

I also give students a rating on their use of time. Sometimes we mistake activity for productivity. Is what we're killing ourselves to do going to matter in eternity?

Another area we look at is working with others. Are we able to get along with people who see it like we do? Can we also get along with those who may rub us the wrong way more than they do the right way?

This next area would seem like a stretch when compared to spiritually, but do we complete our work and do so neatly? God expects our best, not a job half done or done half heartily.

Last but not least, are we polite in our behavior? The bottom line is that behavior is very important, because the world monitors all our actions. They expect more from a Christian than from their own people. The Scripture tells us how to walk and gives us help through the person of the Holy Spirit. If we find we're getting a flunking grade in some of these areas, like we tell the kids at school, we still have time to bring up our grades. After all, "Practice makes perfect" is a pleasant thought for someone who doesn't always gets it right the first time around.

First Thessalonians 2:10, 12 says, "You are witnesses, and God also how devoutly and justly and blamelessly we behaved ourselves among you who believe. That you would walk worthy of God who calls you into His own kingdom and glory."

Holiness

God said, "Be holy as I am holy" in first Peter 1:16. Humans say, "I can't measure up to that. I can never be holy like God." That's a true statement, but being holy isn't something you wear, take off, or put on. It's not something we can work for; it's a process that will continue as we progress through life and end when we take our last breath. Our imperfect being shouldn't be an excuse not to mature, move forward, or become more like God.

We respond to this command in different ways. One way is ignoring it. We can't measure up, so we just act like it doesn't exist. Another way would be to always excuse ourselves for not doing it or refusing to see that anything is wrong with our walk. Or we can just bite the bullet, do what Isaiah in Scripture did, see ourselves as God sees us, and see what we need to do to make a change. Isaiah said he was a man of unclean lips. We need to take inventory of our words, actions, and reactions Then we can see whether they measure up with Scripture. If not, we need to make adjustments. If we do measure up, then we can move on to other areas that may need our attention. God set the bar high, but let's not be guilty of trying to lower it to fit our agendas. We can do this. Let's keep walking in the Spirit so we know what a holy life looks like.

First Peter 1:15–16 says, "But as He who called you is holy, you also be holy in all your conduct. Because it is written, 'Be holy, for I a holy.'"

Beautiful Harmony

When I was reading in Ephesians 4:3 some words stood out to me. *Unity* was one word. It's defined as harmony, one accord, the same. Another word was *bond*, which is defined as binding, covenant, agreement, strong cord. The next word was *peace*, and its definition is tranquility, order, freedom from oppressive thoughts or emotions. The last word that struck me while reading this verse was *endeavor*, which is defined to strive for, or to achieve, to reach or to work with a set purpose.

I love music, especially when there is close harmony to whatever I'm listening to. Wrong notes or singing off key makes for a long song. So according to Scripture, we should work with purpose to keep unity or sing the song of life with others in sweet harmony. If we go off pitch or get out of harmony, we need to be so committed or bound by such a strong cord with others that we'll do our part to get it back on track. It's easier to let others know when they are off tune than to just overlook the fault and try for peace. Will we get off tune, out of beat, and put out some sour notes while going through life with others? Yes, that's life, but the beauty of it is that we can live in unity and harmony with the rest of the choir or people we run into along this journey. Let's make some beautiful music, shall we?

Ephesians 4:3 says, "Endeavoring to keep the unity of the Spirit in the bond of peace."

Hide-and-Seek

It was neat when we played hide-and-seek as kids and won the game when we stumped the seeker by finding the best place to hide. It was nice when the pit bull from next door couldn't see me hiding in the garage; I was very glad for the wall that stood between us. Sometimes there's a pleasant time to head out of town and find a place to hide from the rat race of life for a day or two. A hiding place can mean a place of safety or just renewal.

The Word tells us that God is our hiding place or place of refuge. But to find a hiding place in God, we must be proactive. We must run to Him. He won't force Himself on us. The garage wouldn't have done me any good if I hadn't run to the garage like my tail was on fire when the pit bull jumped the fence. I could have wished I were in the garage. I could have just thought it was an option, but I was all for getting away from what I thought could have been that dog's lunch.

We need to treat the Enemy of our souls the same way I feared the pit bull. We need to run to our strong tower, not just hope the Enemy will stop chasing our tails; we need to decide to go to Jesus for refuge. That hiding place would be all about protection, but God gives us a hiding place for renewal as well. Sometimes we just need to hide away from the stress and problems of just living. How sweet it is to get alone with God, let Him renew our strength, and be filled once again with His Spirit to meet our daily battles. So whatever we're seeking—be it shelter or strength—we can run to our strong tower and find refuge.

Proverbs 18:10 says, "The name of the Lord is a strong tower. The righteous run to it and are safe."

Heart of the Matter

The Word tells us to guard our hearts. When it speaks about things being kept in the heart, that would be what we read, memorize, or recall out of God's Word. That is why it says to hide the Word in our hearts. Memorizing, repeating, or writing down verses help to keep the Word where we can use it, as a sword in our Christian walk. The Word is powerful and very needful in spiritual warfare, while the heart or mind is the battlefield. A battle can be fought in just a thought or an emotion of the heart before it even becomes an action.

When the Bible speaks of keeping things from the heart, it just simply means not letting negative emotions or evidences of the flesh rule or control the heart. Just as the Word says, it will spring out into the open through our actions. Just as we want to be physically heart healthy, it's a great idea to be spiritually heart healthy. When we do whatever it takes to guard our hearts and be spiritually heart healthy, this is like physically getting on the treadmill or elliptical machine. Go ahead and have a heart-healthy day both physically and spiritually.

Proverbs 4:23 says, "Keep your heart with all diligence. For out of it spring the issues of life."

Help or Hindrance

The Word tells us in Daniel 6:4 that the king could find neither fault nor error in him. Before we start to think by the wording in this verse that Daniel might have been Superman, let's see what "no fault or no error" means in this verse. Daniel was trustworthy and honest. He kept the rules, did what he was told, and was dependable. This all spoke of his life lived in the kingdom; no mention is made about his faithfulness to his God. That came later in another story altogether.

It's so important that we live so people can't point a finger at us for not honoring who we work for. We see finger pointing a lot when people cheat the system, lie about their whereabouts, steal from the company, call in sick when they aren't sick, and blast the boss. But really, there is one great way to live out our testimony—when our coworkers can't point to times when we were negligent on the job or lazy, spoke negatively about the organization, lied about being late, failed to clock out, or had sticky fingers.

When they couldn't find a problem with Daniel's work ethic, they started in on his faith in God. Having integrity with God is hard when we don't have it with man. Maybe I'm just talking to the choir here with my readers, but here's just a friendly reminder about how our testimony on the job can be a help or hindrance to the cause of Christ. So kudos to all who have good job evaluations and stand up for God in the workplace.

Daniel 6:4 says, "Then the presidents and princes sought to occasion against Daniel concerning the kingdom; but they could none occasion nor fault, neither was there any error or fault found in him."

Humdrum Moments

We tend to feel like what we do doesn't really matter much. When we don't see results, we tend to think we aren't really making a difference or that it really doesn't matter one way or the other whether we even continue to do what we do. But when we're faithful and consistent in the everyday, humdrum moments, we can make a difference.

People want to see someone who isn't wishy-washy in decision making, someone who is there and dependable, someone who is consistent in his or her walk with Christ. When we do right in the small and insignificant choices, and recognize when we have bigger and weightier decisions to make, this behavior prepares us or when the big problems happen in our lives. When we go through big events like cancer, death, divorce, or anything else that can rock our worlds, then in the next big hurdle we face, we can possess peace. So the more we make it through humdrum living by showing consistent lives, the less we're shaken in the not-so-humdrum times. God will take notice of our faithfulness through the small choices and will be able to trust us in the larger matters. Make humdrum events seem extraordinary.

Matthew 25:21 says, "His lord said to him, 'Well done good and faithful servant, you were faithful over a few things I will make you ruler over many things. Enter into the joy of your Lord.'"

Humor Me

Humor is one way I learn to cope with difficulties in life. Some people say they don't have a sense of humor; therefore, humor can't be a coping tool for them. But everyone has the ability to laugh. I love one translation of a verse in Proverbs, which says, "A cheerful disposition is good for your health; gloom and doom leave you bone tired." Sometimes all we need to do to feel better is to let go and have a good laugh. You may not have a sense of humor, but really life isn't all about cracking jokes or being a stand-up comedian. What's important is being able to laugh at yourself, to see the light side of life, and not to take yourself or life too seriously.

So if someone can make me laugh or smile, he or she has followed the prescription to have a merry heart. God created us with two things that are important for us to survive. One is the longing to be loved, and the other is the desire to be happy. Will we laugh all the time? No. But sometimes our smile helps others, or something we said makes them laugh. Everyone can find some time in a day to return a smile, give a smile, or just throw back the head and laugh. Be someone known for living and laughing out loud.

Proverbs 17:22 says, "A merry heart does good like a medicine. But a broken spirit dries the bones."

Home Sweet Home

Home is pleasant to think about. It's a place that is familiar and safe, and it's where you can be yourself. We sometimes think a home is just brick and mortar, but home can be a relationship, a favorite memory, or a warm and fuzzy feeling. Home could also be in more than one place. It's where you're told to take off your shoes, kick back, and stay awhile. It's awesome when someone has the ability to make you feel at home just by your being with him or her. We don't even have to be related; there's just a feeling of a kindred spirit.

So when people say they want to go home, they don't always mean a place but where they are loved and accepted. The Bible doesn't specifically address the word *home*, but it talks about a house God is preparing for us, and surely it will be the ultimate home. After all, we're just passing through here on our way. So be encouraged, readers. We are almost home.

John 14:3 says, "And if I go and prepare a place for you, I will come again and receive you to Myself. That where I am, there you may be also."

Habit Forming

I went through the drive-through at McDonald's one morning and ordered my usual large coffee with seven creams. There was a long line, and when I reached the window to pay, the lady asked what I had ordered without looking. But before I could answer her, she glanced out and said, "I know you and know exactly what you ordered!" I grinned, paid her my usual $1.07, and left. Did that lady really know me? Not really, but I had done the same thing at the same place so many times. She knew me because of my weekly habit.

I hadn't even gotten out of the driveway before the thought came to me. Wouldn't it be great if others knew us by our spiritual habits? Maybe they know our car leaves every Sunday morning when we go to church. Maybe they know we'd bow our heads to thank God for our food. Here are some other maybes: They know we read the Word and don't just carry it to church. They know how we might react under pressure. They know how we deal in business. They know about our stand on morals. They know our word is good. They know we don't participate in what we used to before we met Christ. They know they can depend on us to be there. Will we mess up at times? Sure, but the bottom line is that we habitually want to do what's right; therefore, this has become a way of life. Just as that woman at the drive-through knew what I would order, so may others look at our lives and see our lives lived, not just some of the time but 24-7 for Christ.

Ephesians 3:17 says, "That Christ may dwell in your hearts through faith, that you, being rooted and grounded in love."

Impossibilites

Right now what is your biggest problem or impossibility? Just as Joshua had his impossibility, the walls of Jericho, we have walls of impossibility as well. The walls of Jericho were massive—in fact, walls inside walls. I visited Jericho when I was privileged to visit the Holy Land, and I was reminded of what a big deal this miracle had to be. It wasn't just a story I had learned about in Sunday school. The wall represents something between us and where we want to be.

Joshua asked the wrong question in chapter 5, when he asked God, "Are you for us or against us?"

God answered, "Neither one!"

The question Joshua should have asked was, "Are we on God's side?" Joshua had to be obedient to the battle plan, as insane as it sounded. So this is what it comes down to in taking down the walls of impossibility in our lives. We must recognize that our job is to be obedient, and God's job is to take care of the walls. Does it make sense to break down some walls of any kind by just marching around them and then shouting and breaking some lamps during the last lap? No, because that isn't how we would do things. But God had to do supernatural tasks to show Israel's enemies that what was being done had to be from a miracle-working God, not from the children of Israel in their own strength. We need to remember that we need to get out of the flesh and operate in the Spirit. Then we can show our enemies that we serve a living and miracle-working God.

Joshua 6:2 says, "And the Lord said to Joshua: 'See! I have given Jericho into your hand, its king, and the mighty men of valor.'"

The Insignificant

Have you ever felt like you're just marking time? The Enemy can make us feel like we aren't making a difference or any progress. But once again, our ability isn't on trial; our availability will make the difference. The Enemy can make someone feel insignificant, but how awesome it is to think of what or who God used in the Bible to do very significant things.

Here are just a few that come to mind: a little boy's lunch (which fed five thousand plus), a stick in Moses's hands, mud placed on a blind man's eyes, a rock in a slingshot, faith that was the size of a mustard seed, a widow's mite, a widow's empty flour barrel, and just a cup of water in Jesus's name. What was important wasn't the lunch but a kid stepping up to offer all he had. It wasn't some dead stick that parted waters but the obedience of the one holding the stick that manifested the power of God. What was important wasn't mud that made the blind man see; it was the One holding the mud. It wasn't a rock that killed a giant of a man but the simple faith of a teen to say, "I can do this."

Moving a mountain doesn't require a bushel of seeds; just a little one will do. A penny didn't turn the head of the head usher that day, but the clink was music to the Master's ear, because He knew the penny was her last one. There was no magic in an old wooden barrel lacking the product needed to bake a cake; the "magic" came with the obedient heart of the cook to keep dipping in. Anything done in Jesus's name, no matter how small or large, will become significant. It just boils down to the fact that we are willing and obedient to God.

First Corinthians 1:26–27 says, "For you see your calling, brethren, that not many wise according to the flesh, not many mighty, not many noble are called. But God has chosen the foolish things of the world to put to shame the wise, and God has chosen the weak things of the world to put to shame the things which are mighty."

What Are You Inhaling?

What kind of air are we breathing? We can be assaulted with some toxic air from a skunk that just got hit, a dead carcass lying in the middle of the road, something toxic burning, burned cookies, the smell of singed hair, and the list is long. These smells make us want to run or cover our noses. On the other side of this coin, nothing smells better than clean sheets, an apple pie baking in the over, that new car smell, your favorite perfume, the candle of your choice burning in the living room, or brownies that are hot and ready to eat. Now those nice aromas make you want to take in very deep breaths.

I attended a women's conference and read the lyrics of a song by Matt Redman called "Your Grace Finds Me" that had the phrase "Breathe in grace, breathe out praise." That well describes what we spiritually inhale and exhale. That could be our test. If we breathe in the right air of grace, then what we exhale will be on the positive, encouraging, or tolerant side. If we inhale grace, then we won't make someone want to run away from us or hurt others. Gentleness is one of the fruit of the Spirit, so let's choose it today. Take a deep breath and with that breath praise our great Creator and leave behind a sweet aroma.

Second Corinthians 2:15 says, "For we are to God the fragrance of Christ among those who are being saved and among those who are perishing."

The Invisible

In 2 Chronicles 32, Hezekiah let the Israelites know they needed to trust God and not worry about the king who wanted to take them all out. But let's be honest. We tend to focus on what's visible, depend on what has skin on, and go with what we know to be true based on previous experience. So totally walking in what we don't see is sometimes difficult. Have we seen flesh fail? Oh yes. Have any of our plans turned south? You bet. Have we ever failed in what we've done, thinking all the while that we've got this? More times than we probably want to admit. So why do we go back to the flesh so easily? Even when we take a problem to God, we might still worry about it, carry it as if it depended on us, and already have planned out what will happen.

It has been said that if we really knew what the power of prayer could do, we wouldn't even consider relying on the flesh for anything. That's easier said than done at times. But just as Hezekiah was the cheerleader, encouraging the children of Israel when all they could see was the very visible Enemy, we can encourage each other to trust in the same God Hezekiah prayed to, not on our arms of flesh. In other words, we should trust in the invisible when the visible looks intimidating. By the way, God used the invisible; He sent angels, not the sword of Israel's army, to take care of the Enemy this time. Let's be pleasantly surprised today when God answers our prayer by means we never planned or thought about.

Second Chronicles 32:8 says, "With him is only the arm of flesh, but with us is the Lord our God to help us and to fight our battles."

Out of My League

An encouraging thought today could be that we don't need to be intimidated. There are different ways we can be intimidated, and this can happen in many different places. One place could be at the gym when we see someone who has a flat stomach and no flab visible anywhere. Maybe another place could be at work, when we're in a room full of people who may have degrees tagged on the ends of their names. Maybe we're with someone who has more money than we do, or we visit someone whose house makes our house seem like a shack.

The list would be different for different people. No matter who you are, maybe you feel small against a certain someone or something in your life. David had a very intimidating situation in his life called Goliath. Compared to the other warriors, he didn't have the right outfit, he wasn't the right size, and he didn't carry the right weapon. But David had the right power source. We can be encouraged when we're reminded in the midst of whatever, or whoever, makes us feel a little intimidated to say what David said to Goliath. He came in the name of the Lord. So there's no need to sweat it when we might feel a little out of our league. We just need to show up with what we've got and let God do the rest.

First Samuel 17:45 says, "But David said to him, 'You come to me using a sword and two spears. But I come to you in the name of the Lord All Powerful, the God of the armies of Israel.'"

Judgment Calls

How many times have we made judgment calls, either aloud or in our heads, and then found out we were so very wrong in our assessment. We do a lot of judging of others, especially in our circle of Christian fellowship. We just need to relax and enjoy ourselves in that fellowship. The Word talks about a diversity of people but one God and one work. We need to let our lives be about what we can do to further the work of God and use what gifts or abilities He has given to us to do just that. After all, we aren't an island; we all need each other, especially as the day of Christ's return gets even closer. The whole body isn't just represented in our own home church but in anyone dotted across the globe who has been adopted into the family of God. Who knows? The very "family member" we pass judgment on might be the very one God uses to help us when we need it most. So let's hop off the judgment seat and go for help and guidance at the mercy seat.

Matthew 7:1–2 says, "Judge not, that you be not judged. For with what judgment you judge, you will be judged; and with the measure you use, it will be measured back to you."

Just a ...

Society may say, "You're just a ... janitor, waitress, farmer, salesman, or secretary," implying that your occupation may not be all that significant. Or sometimes, especially for me, if we don't have a bunch of degrees behind our name, then we can be considered "just a ..." It sounds better if we have some fancy title. So I can really let society set the standard sometimes when I look at my job and what I make. The Enemy can make us feel like we're doing very little, making a very small difference, or working in a dead-end job.

But making a difference doesn't always mean what we do for a living. Sometimes our jobs are just that, a means to survive. But what are we doing that counts for eternity? When we think like that, we're really never "just a ..." God used "just a" fisherman, tax collector, shepherd, carpenter, tent maker, widow, and virgin girl. The Word records their stories outside their jobs. The fisherman preached an awesome sermon on the day that changed history. The tax collector walked with God and recorded miracles we read today. The shepherd killed a giant and became a king. The carpenter became Jesus's earthly father. The tent maker became a great example and wrote epistles we live by today. A widow gave her all and became an example of how we should give today. And the little virgin girl became our Savior's mother here on earth. So what in the world could God record about "just an" English teacher?

God uses us even in mundane moments. We just need to look for those God moments. Maybe our lives won't be recorded in a history book somewhere, but heaven will reveal how that touch, that prayer, or that word all done on earth made all the difference for someone's eternal destiny.

Matthew 25:23 says, "His lord said to him, 'Well done, good and faithful servant.'"

Judgment Day

Someday we will face a final judgment. Even though Christ said He hadn't come to judge and that we weren't to judge, He still judges our actions and reactions right now. This judgment focuses on our behavior, whether we have curses or blessings in our daily walk with Christ. When we pay attention to conviction from God and try to work on it, that is exactly how we have blessing in our lives, not curses. When we refuse to walk in the light revealed to us or to listen or learn about God's Word, then we bring judgment on our lives. Sometimes we just don't want to change anything, but really we have the potential to bring so much blessing, and with that blessing, we could help others instead of balking or digging in our heels in our self-righteous ways. If not for grace, there we would go down the street.

Deuteronomy 28:1–2 says, "Now it shall come to pass, if you diligently obey the voice of the Lord your God, to observe carefully all His commandments; and all these blessings shall come upon you."

Loving-kindness

Sometimes we can be kind, but put some love with that kindness, and it can make all the difference in the world to someone. Kindness may say, "Good morning" to that child who comes through the classroom door, but love will give him or her a hug. Kindness may say, "You did a good job on that test," but love will take the time to recognize the child in front of his or her peers. Kindness will say, "Thank you for that picture" while you're still trying to figure out what exactly it is, but love will hang it up on the wall. Kindness will say, "Happy birthday" to the birthday boy or girl, but love will give him or her special treatment all day long. Kindness will nod at his or her stories, but love will give the child your undivided attention to every word. Kindness will say you appreciate his or her hard work, but love will write it in a note and leave it in his or her desk. Kindness will say, "I love you," but love will show love by your actions.

You get the gist of this one; just fill it in with what fits with your life story. Whatever that may be, just go the second mile and don't stop with kindness. Add love to the mix and make it loving-kindness.

Psalm 103:1, 4 says, "Bless the Lord, O my soul; and all that is within me, bless His holy name. Who redeems your life from destruction, Who crowns you with lovingkindness and tender mercies."

Lessons Learned from a Child

Children can teach us how much patience we have, how much love we give, how much forgiveness we extend, and how much faith we possess. A child can make us crazy one moment, then turn around and make us crack up the next. We can be hard on children, and they will turn around and give us a hug. If people hurt our feelings, we tend to hold a grudge. A child will let the offense go and seek our approval, all in the same twenty minutes of the incident. You can be a repeat offender in having to say, "I'm sorry" to a child, and he or she will immediately accept your apology and forget. We tend to forgive but not forget the situation. A child will just believe, and that is that. But we doubt that what we pray for will come to pass, either by our actions or by our impatience for something to happen. Teach us, Lord, to wait, and to do so with a smile on our faces. Do it the way of a child, because after all, Jesus taught us that we would have to come as a child to enter the kingdom. So there's just something to think about.

Matthew 18:2–3 says, "Then Jesus called a little child to Him, set him in the midst of them. And said, 'Assuredly, I say to you unless you are converted and become as little children, you will by no means enter the kingdom of heaven.'"

Labels

The Bible gives different people in the Bible nicknames or labels we remember them by: Doubting Thomas; Judas, the traitor; Saul, the persecutor; Rahab, the harlot; Peter, the impulsive; Mary Magdalene; the demon possessed; Bartimaeus, the blind man; and the thief on the cross. But then Jesus entered the picture and turned Thomas into a believer. He turned Saul to Paul, Peter to a rock, a harlot to someone who landed on the family tree of the Messiah, a demon-possessed woman to a Spirit-filled follower of Christ, a blind man to someone with twenty-twenty vision, and a thief deserving death to a forgiven soul who saw paradise. So the next time we're tempted to stick a label on someone, we should stop and consider what labels we could wear if not for the grace of God.

Psalm 84:11 says, "For the Lord God is a sun and shield; the Lord will give grace and glory. No good thing will He withhold from those who walk uprightly."

Love versus Fear

Why do we give our lives to Christ? Some do it to get out of a tight spot; others may do it for the attention they receive from people. Others may do it because someone else decided to follow Christ, and others may do it because they don't want to go to hell. I guess being scared into a relationship with Christ can be good, but what a difference it can make when we make the decision because He loves us. We can do nothing in return except love Him back. To decide to have a relationship with God out of fear is like giving a hug without that hug being returned.

Following Christ out of fear makes a rule keeper instead of a joy giver. Do I want to go to hell? Of course not, but I want to love my God because I know He loves me, not because I have the fear of hell hanging over my head. If we choose to follow Christ because of the love element, then we won't be so apt to be in and out, up and down, and spiritually wishy-washy. We may be spiritually established, but sometimes we let our love grow cool when we allow life and what happens to distract us. So this is just a reminder to love God not because we have to but because we want to.

Second Timothy 1:7 says, "For God has not given us a spirit of fear; but of power and of love and of a sound mind."

Live in the Moment

We can live in the present and enjoy each moment, but we want to worry about the future; and in so doing, we can miss moments happening right in front of us. These are moments to make memories we won't be able to get back to later. We can be so stressed about something that it can cause us to miss out on enjoying something in the present. A negative outlook about something can also overshadow a moment, and we fail to see it as something to be enjoyed. Then some people are too busy looking back or remembering past regrets that they fail to look at just today and seize that moment. After all, we can live only one day at a time, and we won't ever get this day back. So live in the moment and make some present-day and present-moment memories.

James 4:14 says, "Whereas you do not know what will happen tomorrow. For what is your life? It is even a vapor that appears for a little time and then vanishes."

Is Our Loaf Moldy?

One Sunday I opened my children's church box, and the loaf of bread I was using as a visual aid was green with mold. Obviously it was no longer useful to me as a teaching tool. Then one Sunday night I asked my friend what the pastor had preached about, since I hadn't made it to church that night and needed a word. She told he hadn't preached, so I had better open up my own Bible.

The lesson learned is that we need to get fresh words from the Word every day, and we can't depend on someone else to give them to us. I could have used the moldy bread and fed it to the kids, but they wouldn't have wanted green bread, and I wouldn't have wanted to make them sick. But we want to operate in the spiritual realm with a moldy loaf of bread. We can't be content with past blessings; those are for only the day we received them. We need to have something fresh and new from God. When we're going on the same blessing we received yesterday, last week, or even last month, it's moldy and makes our testimony unattractive and ineffective. Even the children of Israel had to learn this lesson in the wilderness, when they were instructed to pick up only enough manna for that day, or it would go bad.

So when we need to think back to a time when God gave us something from His Word or when we really feel a fresh touch from God, that would be our heads-up that we need to fill our spiritual tank with time spent with God. Sometimes the daily routine of life—yes, even doing ministry—sucks our tanks dry. I'm thankful for my friend's wise response to my desire for a shortcut from the Word. Let's get in the Word and let the Word get in us.

Revelation 3:15–16 says, "I know your works, that you are neither cold not hot. I could wish you were cold or hot. So then because you are lukewarm, and neither cold nor hot, I will spew you out of My mouth."

Life's Not Fair

If you live long enough, you will soon find out that rain falls on the just and the unjust, and sometimes it doesn't just rain; it pours. But it's what we do with all that rain in our lives that counts. Some use the water to grow, while others curse the water and wait to go under. Some find the life preserver, while others complain that it doesn't fit. Some get in the boat and get to where they need to go, while others miss the boat, whining that they'd rather take the bus.

So when life happens, and it will, do whatever it takes to stay afloat and throw a life preserver to the one who may be going down for the third time. If we know Christ, we know He did that for us when He gave His life. Who knows? He may just want us to walk on the water given to us. But for sure be encouraged that the sun is shining behind the clouds. Rest in the fact that we have flood insurance in Jesus whenever we see the rainbow stretched across our cloudy skies.

Matthew 5:45 says, "That you may be sons of your Father in heaven; for He makes His sun rise on the evil and on the good, and sends rain on the just and on the unjust."

What a Difference a Day Makes

What a difference a day can make. Some people woke up with their dreams dashed when they found out their little one wouldn't see this side of heaven. Some people woke up to having to make funeral arrangements for their newborn instead of starting a college fund. Some people woke up with the uncertainty of whether medical help would stop or slow their death sentence. Some people woke up this morning, celebrating another year of birth and the hope of a long life. Some people woke up, looking forward to soon tying the knot. Some people woke up beside someone they had taken for granted, while others woke up with someone they couldn't imagine living without. Some people woke up with no regrets at the present moment, while others wished for a do over. Some people woke up with hope that there is still life, even when this one doesn't play out like they wanted it to.

A long time ago someone lived, was falsely accused, and was killed for living a holy, decent life. Hope was all but gone; it looked like evil had won. But what a difference a day can make. It was Friday, but Sunday came. Life isn't always fair, but because of our hope in Christ, we can make it through those days that can forever change our lives. Sometimes hope is all we have, but really it's all we need.

Romans 5:2–4 says, "And rejoice in hope of the glory of God. And not only that, but we also glory in tribulations, knowing that tribulation produces perseverance, and perseverance, character; and character, hope."

Coming in Second Place

Life isn't about how you win but how you lose. I'm very competitive when I play anything. Hence, I love to win a whole lot better than I like to lose. It's important when we're playing and really in it for blood that we remember it's just a game. Life is going to be filled with competition, and I'm just talking about sports and games. We will find competition in the church, in the home, in relationships, on the job, and anywhere else we may go. There is a mentality of me against you in the world.

It's only human to want to be the best or want the promotion or want to get ahead or just come in first place. The disciples even did this when they vied for the best place beside the Master. But just as we aren't always winners at the end of the game, we will at times come in second place. But the Word says that to gain our lives, we must first lose them. To appreciate gain, we will have to see some loss, and to be first, we will have to be content with being last. But in the end we will all be winners.

Matthew 20:16 says, "So the last will be first, and the first last. For many are called, but few chosen."

Modern-Day Miracles

I taught a section about miracles in our children's church one month. We went over miracles and other awesome events in the Bible. The list included the following: parting of the Red Sea, feeding a crowd with just a small lunch, men being thrown into a furnace but not burning, a man not being eaten alive by lions, a kid taking down a man three times his size with only a slingshot, water being turned into wine for a party, speaking to rocks to get water, a talking donkey, blind eyes seeing, deaf ears hearing, dead people coming back to the land of the living, walking on water, a fish swallowing a man who lives to talk about it—and that's just a short list. We could be tempted to ask, "What is so great about this day and age?"

I loved it when our church had cardboard testimonies—when people didn't say a word but instead just lifted up a card with words stating before Christ actions, and flipping the card to words stating after Christ actions. The poster board telling us their story of where they had been and where they were now. Homes were restored, alcoholics became sober, drug addicts were clean, the broken were mended, and the prodigal came home; there were healings of all kinds. People shed their old ways, the old places where they used to hang out, and their old friends, who weren't going in the same direction they were. They cleaned up their lifestyles, their speech, and their minds. People who had once been as lost as could be were now pastors, children's workers, youth workers, and faithful church members. Our needs were met, and even when we didn't see a way, God made a way. Someone got a diagnosis that looked bad, but God stepped in and changed it.

So the next time we're tempted to think miracles don't happen today, just look at where we came from and compare that to where we are right now. Thank God for His power to change, deliver, and save.

Second Corinthians 5:17 says, "Therefore, if anyone is in Christ, he is a new creation; old things have passed away. Behold all things have become new."

Motives of the Heart

Are we more concerned about what people say or think about us than about what God thinks or knows about us? The older we become, we don't have the same level of caring what others think about of us. But sometimes in certain cases we revert back to caring to the point that it might override what God knows about us.

God knows exactly who we are and what our motives are all the time. He knows who we are in the light and the dark. He knows our hearts and desires. He knows whether we're sincere. There's nothing wrong with being concerned about what people think, but the Enemy can turn this into something negative because it becomes a never-ending job of making people happy. At the judgment everything will be about us before Him, so it should make us want to sit up and take note of what He would like changed in our character.

We humans can be fickle; for instance, today the world may think we're the cat's meow, but just wait. By tomorrow, we will be on their hit list. But the Word says in Hebrews that Christ is the same all the time. God changes not, so there's more reason we need to be concerned with what He thinks about us. He doesn't change what He wants or thinks. We can change what He commands us to do to fit our life, but that doesn't change God's Word one iota.

Hebrews 13:8 says, "Jesus Christ is the same yesterday, today, and forever."

Drop the Act

We can be free to be ourselves, but on one day of the year, called Halloween, people try to become someone they really aren't. They use Halloween as a good excuse to hide behind a mask. For one day, a little kid can be whatever his or her little heart desires.

As born-again children of God, however, we're free to be our own unique selves. We don't need to hide behind a disguise that covers up who we really are or how we feel about ourselves. We don't need to live in bondage of trying to be happy or to let on to the world that everything is great when our lives are really a mess. It's so freeing to know who we are in Christ and what that means when we know that fact. Blessed is the person who can be candid but tactful, who can be totally honest but not hurtful, and who can tell it like it is but not tear down. Being redeemed, we aren't bound to wearing a mask beyond the day called Halloween. At the end of the day, the mask will go away, and we can live a life free of disguise.

Romans 8:2 says, "For the law of the Spirit of life in Christ Jesus has made me free from the law of sin and death."

Maturity Level

We know we're growing in the Lord if we don't lose control. That may sound a bit unclear, but when we're always in drama mode whenever something goes wrong, that's a sure sign that we need to grow stronger spiritually. Another way to monitor our progress is by seeing what is driving us over the edge. In other words, are we stressing out and losing it over something that won't matter one iota or make one bit of difference in the morning?

There are things in our lives that could make us tremble on the rock, but we can always look around and see that others have something that is a lot harder to deal with than the stressor for our day. I love to see a mature Christian who walks in quiet confidence that God is in control of whatever is going on in his or her life. I find it a lot easier to be around drama-free people. I tend not to be as sympathetic as I should be when they are forever in one crisis after another. Drama-filled people are in the habit of getting up and finding something to create, whatever doesn't cause harmony.

This story illustrates my point: I had a child in my classroom who had an artificial leg. She came up to my desk to tell on herself. She said she'd hit her artificial leg on the desk and yelled out like she was in pain. She thought, *That didn't hurt. That is my fake leg.*

This is a lot like life. People are so in the habit of complaining, being negative, and just seeing the dark side all the time that they yell out for nothing. We would be better off and much further down the road spiritually if we were in the habit of leaving everything in God's hands, living drama free, and having a quiet confidence that our God has it all under control.

Isaiah 40:28–29 says, "Have you now known? Have you not heard? The everlasting God, the Lord, the Creator of the ends of the earth, neither faints nor is weary. His understanding is unsearchable."

Missed Opportunities

How many times do we find great opportunities to share Christ? How many times are we late or in a hurry, so we let the opportunity pass? Or maybe we're hesitant because we feel incapable or scared of what another person may think of us, so the opportunity is gone. We've heard it said many times that what we do is much more important than what we say, because someone is always looking on at our actions and reactions, and listening to the words we give to others. Showing the love of Christ is very hard when we've just chewed out the lady in the drive-through for not getting our order right. It's hard to share the love of Christ when we're complaining and grumbling to the one we want to invite to church with us. It's hard to show the love of Christ when we're laying on the horn for someone to get going at the traffic light.

Confession is good for the soul, so let me share an example with one of my drives home from school. I hate it when I can't make the light on one of the off-ramps in Wichita, Kansas. So if people aren't moving on, they get on my nerves. One evening the light was green, but the first car wasn't moving. I told him to go from inside my car, as if he could hear me. Then I saw him open his door, get out, and give money to a guy holding a sign on the side of the road. Boy, did I feel like a heel.

Not only is confession good, but so is conviction. I shot an apology heavenward for yelling at a driver who never knew I existed; he never saw me not acting Christlike in traffic. That driver didn't miss his opportunity to help someone. We need to walk carefully through life so we don't miss golden opportunities God calls His appointments.

Ephesians 5:15–16 says, "See then that you walk circumspectly, not as fools but as wise. Redeeming the time, because the days are evil."

Nobody Gave You That Bad Mood

We can be in a bad mood for various reasons. We overslept and were late for work. A headache kicked our tails. Our least favorite person just walked in the room. Our day didn't go as planned. Someone said something negative about us. Our car didn't start, and later we had a flat tire. We left our phone at home. Menopausal moments happened. We slammed on the brakes, and coffee went all over the car.

Yes, all these events can be aggravating, but they aren't problems that can't be fixed, changed, or just gotten over by changing our thoughts to something more positive. We need to remember that no one or nothing gave us that bad mood; we just took it and ran with it. It's better being late for work than not having a job. A headache can be uncomfortable to work with, but we haven't gotten a diagnosis of cancer. That one person isn't our favorite can't compare to the long list of great friends we enjoy. Plans are good, but if we don't carry them out, our world won't go flying off its axis. Car trouble just lets us be thankful that we at least own a car. Menopause is just another bump in the road of growing older.

So let's ask help from our Creator, who designed us in the first place to grow older with grace, and not be known as Grumpy Pants. I plan to make it to heaven one way or another, and I mean to enjoy the trip. We can make the trip more enjoyable for us and others if we let God have our moods.

Psalm 16:11 says, "You will show me the path of life. In Your presence is fullness of joy. At Your right hand are pleasures forevermore."

We Can't Do It All

There's a lesson in being able to say no every once in a while. Sometimes we take on too much, and this burden tends to overwhelm us, or we take on other people's problems because they pick us to be their counselor. Then their problems add to our own stress. But it's better to dodge a ball coming at us than to catch it or commit ourselves to a task and end up dropping the ball, not getting it done, or not doing the task well. We tend to overbook ourselves, and something or someone will always suffer for this way of planning. It ends up that balls are in the air, bouncing off walls and out of control.

We need to stop and use wisdom in how to catch a ball, meaning to get involved but not to the point of burnout. We can be a help to others but not let this burden suck the joy out of our spirits. So happy are those who have figured out which balls to catch (to commit to), to dodge (to say no to), or to drop (to walk away from).

Proverbs 4:5 says, "Get wisdom! Get understanding from the words of my mouth."

Nurturing Isn't for the Faint of Heart

I was reading one day and came across an article about nurturing plants. It was odd that I was even interested, since I don't have a single plant in my possession. I tend to kill them, not nurture them. But really, we do that nurturing thing all the time with our kids, grandkids, kids at school, kids at church, or wherever a relationship is involved. We can nurture in many ways; some are good, and some are not so good. For example, we can nurture by ignoring the situation, such as a hard relationship, and hoping it will go away. We can nurture by smothering the situation or by not allowing God to move in His own way or time. We can nurture by rushing the growth. Or we can just relax and nurture with a gentle and caring spirit.

No, I'm not referring to plants now but to anyone God allows to come into our lives who needs our compassion and spiritual nurturing. Not everyone is going to be an easy nurturing assignment. We might even want to give up on a relationship or two. But then we get those who come into our lives and bloom after we've nurtured them; that experience makes it worth staying with the more stubborn ones. They come in all forms. There are family members, friends, complete strangers, or the one standing in front of us throughout a day. We can make it a priority to find a "plant" who needs nurturing. We never know where we will come in the process. We may be the planter or the one who waters, but for sure we need to be one or the other so God can see to the growth in every situation.

First Corinthians 3:6 says, "I planted, Apollos watered, but God gave the increase."

I Found My Niche

How many times have we heard that someone is "a natural"? Such wording is an affirmation to that person that he or she has found his or her calling, niche, gift, talent, or ability in whatever he or she does at the time. Sometimes we fall into being "a natural" by accident. We really weren't planning something, but life happened, and we did something and found out we weren't half bad at it. Then other times we trained for something and ended up having the ability to continue something as a gift. Sometimes the activity was a necessary evil to be done, and we ended up being what God used to push us into what we needed to be involved in.

But then there was the time when we knew it from the get-go. We came out with an ability in our DNA, and as we matured, that thing blossomed within us. But really it doesn't matter how the ability came to be; it is God's design that we use it to bring glory to Him and help to others. When that happens, then it brings contentment to us. So our happy place can be our niche cut out especially for us.

First Corinthians 12:4–6 says, "There are diversities of gifts, but the same Spirit. There are differences of ministries, but the same Lord. And there are diversities of activities, but it is the same God who works all in all."

What to Overlook

Sometimes other people bug us. Annoyances come up and make us say things or tote an attitude around, when probably we need to use wisdom and just try to move on and overlook something. Wisdom tells us whether it will really matter or whether it will affect us or others. Sometimes we ride other people about things that really don't need to be brought up or brought to someone's attention. Sometimes some of the things that drive us nuts may be the very things we do in our own lives.

For example, one day I had my loudest kid in class that year, and he got into trouble the most for causing distractions; he came up to my desk and asked me to tell another child to be quiet, because he couldn't concentrate. I thought it was ironic that the most distracting child in class was at my desk, complaining that another child was distracting him. But I just told him, "Well, now you know what it's like when you're being loud and making it hard for others to concentrate." He hated the very thing he'd done on a regular basis.

Maybe that's why some people bug us so much; they do the things we hate most about ourselves. Just as I wanted the child in my classroom to overlook the other child for disrupting his focus, so should we be more compassionate with people and their ways. The Lord knows I have flaws I hope others will overlook. With that said, we know God doesn't overlook sin; neither should we. So once again, wisdom is the art of knowing what's a sin or just a pet peeve. For if it's sin, then we have a responsibility to take care of that in our lives and use wisdom to take care of it in other's lives if it affects us. May God give us wisdom to know when to sit on it, stand up, or shut up.

Proverbs 19:11 says, "The discretion of a man makes him slow to anger, and his glory is to overlook a transgression."

Outward versus Inward

We tend to look at others and say, "Wow, they really have it together!" But we're going on only the outward appearance, when really the truth of the matter is that they are a mess inside.

I once bought a car that was sharp on the outside, but let me tell you that it turned out to be the biggest lemon on the car lot. It left me stranded on the side of highways. I towed it to Florida when I moved there; I'm pretty sure it wouldn't have made the trip otherwise. I loaned it out for a day, and it came back with smoke coming from under the hood. The mechanic told me to just get it running and get rid of it. It looked good on the outside, but it wasn't what I thought it would be: a nice car that would keep going like the Energizer bunny. It had been cheap, and I had thought it was a bargain, but the repairs nearly bankrupted me.

Although you want your car to look good as you drive it off the lot, what counts is what's under the hood. God looks at the heart, and man looks at the outside appearance. The two perceptions can be very different indeed. God knows what we are, so there's no need to try deceiving ourselves to think God will never know. Walk your truth today, and others will see a person who is the same inside and out.

First Samuel 16:7 says, "God does not see the same way people see. People look at the outside of a person, but the Lord looks at the heart."

"This Ain't It"

"This ain't it!" That little sentence with a grammatical error speaks volumes to me. When life gets monotonous or a little discouraging, remember that "this ain't it." When we worry about the future or whether we'll have enough money to retire or just survive, remember that "this ain't it." When our bodies let us down with added pains and we find that doing things we used to do is harder, we need to remember that "this ain't it." When we see the social decline in morals and so much compromise going on, we need to remember that "this ain't it." When we get a bad diagnosis, receive an answer we didn't want to hear, or are disappointed with those we love, we need to keep in mind that "this ain't it."

Just go to the last chapter in the Bible and read where all things will become new. Yes, this world will soon be over, but until then, we have Someone who has promised not to let us down. We have His Word to guide us, the Holy Spirit to comfort us, and life within us to help us not to have to experience a horrible existence on earth. But we have as much of heaven right here and right now as possible. That last chapter also tells us that we win.

Revelation 22:3 says, "And there shall be no more curse, but the throne of God and of the Lamb shall be in it and His servants shall serve Him."

Let God Call the Shots

Next door to grace, peace is a very important commodity to have in our Christian walk. One would think that if we have Christ, we have peace. But many children of God run around without this fruit of the Spirit. When someone who is in Christ exhibits this gift, you will see his or her ability to remain faithful, even when everyone around him or her is giving in. That person doesn't live in panic mode, even though the panic button would have been very easy to push in many situations. There's a calm about him or her, but that's not to say there's never trouble brewing. But in the midst of trouble, chaos, and anxiety, that person has peace.

The Bible talks about letting the peace of God rule in our hearts. Two words jump out at me: *peace* and *rule*. When I think of the word *peace*, I think of somewhere quiet and serene. Nothing makes a disturbance of any kind. The other word is *rule*. We've learned that another word for *rule* is *umpire*. We can understand that because we attend ball games; we know who calls the shots and has the last say. That's the umpire.

So peace in the Bible doesn't speak of ten days spent on a Hawaiian beach, although that would paint a picture of peace to me. It doesn't even speak of a life absent of troubles. Let God be our umpire, let Him call the shots, let Him have the final say, and let Him be the mediator of the Enemy of our peace, because God give us peace *in* our troubles, not *out* of troubles. Just as the umpire is needed so the ball game doesn't get out of control, so it's important that we let God be the One who keeps the peace and doesn't allow situations, others, or even ourselves to get out of control. Our peace will be disturbed; we can always count on that. But we can also count on God to provide peace in the middle of life by doing what the Word says: by keeping our minds focused on Christ. Then He gives us perfect peace.

Colossians 3:15 says, "Let the peace of God rule in your hearts."

Push the Pause Button

One day God used one of my unruly kids as a visual aid to teach me patience. Here are the lessons I learned that day:

1. Let the child finish his or her sentences before responding. Don't assume what he or she is going to say.
2. Wait to respond or don't respond if your words will come out as a negative response.
3. Don't let your body language speak of what you're really thinking. That would include the eye roll, the shake of the head, or the exasperated sigh.
4. See the child as one of God's workmanship, who is still in progress. (God knows I'm an unfinished project under construction.)
5. Pray for the child and take the situation to God instead of always bringing it up with others or even letting it play over and over in your head.
6. Don't analyze the child. Love him or her. Notice that just about every lesson mentioned above involves pausing, listening, and pausing again. Pausing has a lot to do with having the fruit of the Spirit called patience. Sometimes by pushing the pause button, you can eliminate having to push the delete button for word, actions, or reactions that wouldn't have happened if you'd just paused.

James 1:4 says, "But let patience have its perfect work, that you may be perfect and complete, lacking nothing."

Living inside the Hedge

If we stay in Christ, then we're protected. In the Word we read about battles or other stories about people who didn't obey the command of God; they went down in defeat. Defeat may have been losing all their possessions, their lives, or the battle; but lose they did. Over and over God promised to protect Israel, but they had to stay under the protection of being obedient. But there were those who became greedy and went rogue. God's protection doesn't mean no trouble, disease, or death; just ask Job in the Old Testament. But we're protected from evil in this messed-up world where we live.

We leave God's protection by being disobedient, sinning willfully, or just not being able to play well with others in the church body; hence we get ticked off, refuse to forgive, or get bitter—all reasons that cause one to live on the edge of that protection. It's like not coming out of the rain, as it were, and enjoying the secure feeling of having a hedge of protection about us. The devil can cross that hedge line only with God's permission. Satan may touch us physically, but he's off limits when it comes to our spirits and souls.

So can we be secure in our salvation? You better believe it, if we stay under God's protection and inside the hedge He places around our souls. Even Satan recognized that Job had a hedge all around him. I like it when God asked Satan whether he had noticed his servant Job. Some think, *Oh no, here it comes because God says that.* But I think, *What a comfort it is for the God of the universe to notice me.* Take heart; the God of the universe has us covered, and we're in His sights for His protection.

Job 1:10 says, "Have You not made a hedge around him, around his household, and around all that he has on every side? You have blessed the work of his hands, and his possessions have increased in the land."

Someone Only a Mother Could Love

It has been said that we will love Jesus as much as the person we love the least. My mind immediately goes to the one person I probably love the least in this world, and I think, *Oh boy, am I in trouble.* Seriously, we don't have to like someone or his or her ways, but we can still love that person in spite of it all, because God knows I'm someone only a mother could love at times. If we're walking in the Spirit, He gives us a love we wouldn't have if we were operating in the flesh. Our human mind would say, "No, I can't love that person." So it's very important that we operate and walk in the Spirit so we can love people, serve them, and put them before ourselves. When that happens, we find that whatever it is that makes our human part want to run instead of love that part won't rear up and show its ugly head, because regardless of whether we agree with the opening statement, the Word tells us that we can't say we love God and despise His children.

Matthew 5:23–24 says, "Therefore if you bring your gift to the altar and there remember that your brother has something against you, leave your gift there before the altar, and go your way. First be reconciled to your brother and then come offer your gift."

Passion

Other words for *passion* are *zeal, intense enthusiasm, overpowering emotions*, or *concentrated interest*. We all have passion, even if we want to think we don't. We have a zeal for sports, an intense enthusiasm for cooking or crafts, overpowering emotions for anything that makes us happy, or a concentrated interest in keeping our bodies fit and toned. To say we really don't get excited about anything isn't usually the norm.

Often when someone in the Bible was commended for something, having a passion for God and His work usually made the list. To be a passionless Christian is an oxymoron. Christ showed passion by leaving paradise and coming to earth to be born, to walk among us, and to take our sins when He died on the cross. He showed us how life is done. He did so with passion. Dying for sinners would have been hard unless He had some passion.

So the least we could do in return is to live with passion. Our zeal for God should match the passion we have for things here on earth. What a testimony to leave behind for our family and friends that we had a zeal for God. When we live passionless lives or lives not focused on God, we fight a losing battle and can be deceived that all is well. So let's pray that God will give us a passion for Him and His work that will exceed the passions we have for our favorite things here on earth.

Romans 10:2 says, "For I bear them witness that they have a zeal for God."

Our Help Is Just a Prayer Away

I love the song "Help Is within the Reach of a Prayer." I read a journal entry I wrote that said, "God is really answering prayer for my friend. I think that is so cool." I don't remember which friend or even what the prayer was that was answered, but the entry again reminded me of the power of prayer. A prayer can be just a short, whispered plea given in the moment when something becomes urgent in our day. A prayer can be something we do throughout a day as someone or something comes to our minds. Sometimes prayer is a marathon when we have prayed a long time for a person or situation. Prayer can be a venting session with God when we tell Him what He already knows, but we need to get it out of our system. Prayer is a time of worship when we let Him know we're blessed and how grateful we are for our blessings.

So it's very encouraging when we see answers to prayer, and it's also encouraging to hear that someone took the time to mention our name to the Father. It just might be the prayer that changes that person's day for the good. I know we all have said it one time or another: "I will pray for you." But sometimes we say this and don't think about it again.

I have a friend in Missouri who doesn't just say those words; she stops right there and prays with the person. I also have a spiritual mentor who writes down her prayers. One day when I really needed it, she let me know she had written a prayer for me. Jesus told Peter in Luke 22:31-32 that He'd prayed for Him so Satan wouldn't sift him as wheat. Wow, you can't get a better person to pray for you than Jesus. Remember, fellow reader, that Jesus prays and intercedes for us at the right hand of the Father. So help is closer than you think.

James 5:16 says, "The effective, fervent prayer of a righteous man avails much."

It's All in How You Look at It

How does God perceive us? One weekend I was out of town and staying in a motel. On Sunday morning I sat in the breakfast area, talked to people, and watched them. I saw a group I would call a motley crew, probably in their twenties. They wore tattoos, were gothic, and had pierced, punk hairdos; and yes, they smelled like they needed baths. I listened to them talk, and they didn't use the best choice of words. One talked about someone who had obviously done her wrong. They weren't particular about who listened in, because everyone within earshot could hear what they said. They were a group of people I must admit I didn't care to start up a conversation with, so I didn't.

Then there was the woman who tried to carry two coffees. She dropped some other things she was carrying, and I immediately asked whether I could take her coffee for her. She said, "Just find the bald man and set it down there."

I grinned and said, "I better not address him as the bald man," and she just laughed. I turned, and the bald man was also a black man. I later thought, "Some would see 'black.' She saw 'bald,' but what does God see?" I saw tattoos, piercings, and outlandish hairdos, but what does God see?

God sees someone made in His image with a soul who will live forever. Jesus didn't just talk with the ones who were easy to chat with. He didn't just help those whom He got along with the best. He didn't pick and choose whom He would help. He was there for everyone.

On the way home, I talked with a friend about those encounters at the breakfast nook. It seems that we like to label people, so then it's harder to see how God sees them with that label hanging around their necks. We start with assuming something, and then that thinking works its way to the end of that spectrum, called judging. When we get there, we're of no use to God, because we try to do what only

God can—to judge. We need to be able to look beyond what a person looks like, how he or she smells, or even what we perceive to be his or her problem. As the saying goes, "Everyone is someone's child." Look at the world from God's perspective, which is centered on a man's soul.

Luke 19:10 says, "For the Son of Man has come to seek and to save that which was lost."

Our Daily Appointment with God

With one look at our calendars, it's evident that we have too many appointments. Sometimes we forget an appointment, or we're late and have to reschedule. Sometimes we go but really don't look forward to that appointment; for me that would be going to the dentist. Other appointments make us smile, like sharing a cup of java with a friend. But we keep some appointments because they are our duty or a necessary evil, like having a colonoscopy. Our appointment with God is so important. Some people have problems keeping their appointment with God; then they wonder why life is out of control for them.

Some appointments don't really matter if we blow them off. But we will soon find out that not keeping our appointment with God will show up in our actions and words. Not only do we need to show up, but we need to be proactive in our appointments. In other words, we need to pay attention to what God shows us during those times and be doers, not just hearers, of the Word. In other words, we should just keep these appointments because they are our duty; we should keep them, knowing they are our spiritual lifeline. The Word tells us over and over again that Jesus needed to keep His appointment with His Father. If Jesus needed to do this, how much more do His children need to find time for their daily appointment with God.

Luke 5:16 says, "So He Himself [Jesus] often withdrew into the wilderness and prayed."

Relationships

To have a good relationship with anyone, we must work on becoming the right kind of person. So we can become the right kind of friend, employee, child, parent, boss, teacher, or spouse. The is a long list of different kinds of relationships. We always have in our heads what the perfect husband, perfect student, perfect child, or perfect church member would be like, compared to whatever we are actually matched up with. But we leave out of the equation the other person in the relationship, and that would be us. If we want mercy, we have to show mercy; if we want to be loved, we have to show love; if we want affirmation, we need to quit criticizing. If we want justice, we need to put away our judgmental spirit. If we want patience shown to us, we must have grace.

So how do we become that right person for whatever relationship? The Word tells us to live the right way, serve God, and walk in the Spirit. We stay in the Word, keep a good communication with our Maker, and let the Spirit have permission to flow through us. This is a daily process, something we will forever improve in this life. Also the Word gave us a prime example of what having good relationships looks like by letting us meet Ruth.

The story of Ruth speaks of loyalty and commitment. We think it has a lot to do with choosing a mate, but everyone needs that kind of person in his or her corner. The culture teaches us that if you're pretty or handsome, if you have money, if you do all the "right" things in someone's eyes, then the other person will be loyal. But just gain a few pounds, run out of money, and quit making the cut anymore; then watch his or her so-called loyalty walk out the door. Our list may be long of whom we consider to be a friend, but the list becomes even shorter when we highlight the ones who've stayed by the stuff in the good, the bad, and the ugly. We need to pray and thank God for those who are not only on the list but also in our corner.

Ruth 1:16 says, "And Ruth said, 'Entreat me not to leave you, or to return from following after you. For wherever you go, I will go, where you will lodge, I will lodge, your people shall be my people, your God my God.'"

R & R

This subject, R & R, can be a very religious thing to do. God in all His wisdom even put R & R on His list of things to create. R & R does a body good and the spirit good as well. The body was wired to include this religious exercise. When we practice it, we renew our bodies, souls, and minds. The Enemy may try to take it from us, because he knows that when we don't get it, we aren't very useful, productive, or even civil. When we don't do R & R, our perspective becomes cloudy, our patience becomes nonexistent, our productivity is hampered, our reactions are laced with overkill, our words are a mite sharp, and our minds are overwhelmed and busy with thoughts that keep us from doing what God admonishes His creation to do. Sometimes our physical bodies make it hard for us to get plenty of what I'm talking about accomplished. Pain, worry, schedules, and to-do lists also keep R & R from happening.

How is rejecting rest spiritual? God gave us an example by resting on the seventh day, Jesus Himself found the need to get away from it all and rest. When we are physically rested, our spiritual man feels renewed as well. Sometimes the most spiritual thing for us to do is just to go to sleep. So take that vacation or get away for the weekend. Just take a nap and see whether everything will look a whole lot better after some downtime.

Hebrews 4:9 says, "There remains therefore a rest for the people of God."

Romanticism

I have two friends, a brother and sister, both of whom teach English at the same school in Olathe, Kansas. She is a great writer and wrote about an occasion in the classroom when her students were actually catching on to her lecture; she wrote eloquently about this on Facebook. Her brother, a big tease, wrote about a kid who went to sleep during his lecture. He then said, "I am a realist, and my sister is a romantic." In other words, kids don't usually sit up and drink in your every word in the real world, but maybe in a world that overlooks what the norm is, they will. That way of thinking is called romanticism in literature.

But I think it's fine to be a romantic thinker in the Christian life as well. In the real world people get sick, die, get divorced, break hearts, disappoint, commit crimes, and make bad decisions. The devil always steals and destroys. But sometimes we need to see the other side—that kids do get it sometimes, some make good decisions, people are healed, people are still true blue, there are still couples growing old together, and God is still in control. All things that happen in the "real" world will soon be over. So let's keep our minds on what a non-Christian might think would be spiritual "romanticism" and hold fast to the hope we have in Christ.

Colossians 3:1–2 says, "If then you were raised with Christ, seek those things which are above, where Christ is, sitting at the right hand of God. Set your mind on things above, not on things on the earth."

How We Will Be Remembered

In one year I lost four family members. This experience really got me to thinking about how fragile life is. Not to be morbid, but one day will be our last. How we want to be remembered should be on our minds. Are we better or bitter, positive or negative, loving life or dreading each day? Are we joy givers or joy suckers, loving or hateful, servants or selfish, generous people or tightwads, helpful or a hindrance, riding the bus or going under the bus? I think you get my drift.

But how we are remembered isn't all about how life happened on just one day; it's about how we behaved or lived on a collection of days. Remember, practice makes perfect, and keeping it up makes a habit, and a habit becomes a way of life. Let's live our lives like we're a new creation in Christ. I know it isn't all about how we behave that makes us redeemed children of God, but the evidence that we are children of God will leak out through our words, actions, and reactions. Those will, in turn, tell the world whether we're Christians. We can be remembered that we just survived life or, better yet, that we lived life out loud.

Psalm 16:11 says, "You will show me the path of life. In Your presence is fullness of joy. At Your right hand are pleasures forevermore."

Random Questions

Here are some random questions to consider. What would it be like if we could know exactly what God wants because we have a spiritual GPS system? How would we spend our day if we knew we had only twenty-four hours left? What prayer would we pray if we had only one prayer left that God would answer? Up to this point in our lives, what choice have we made that we would change if possible? If we were given a million dollars, how would we spend it? If we could have chosen our dream job, what would we be doing right now? If we could have a face-to-face conversation with Jesus for forty-five minutes, what would we talk about? If we had to lose one of our five senses, which one would we give up? If we could take only one thing into solitary confinement, what would we choose? If we could pick our spiritual gift, which one would top our list? If we were told that we couldn't read the Bible, which verses would we remember to get us through? If right now we had only one more chance to lead someone to Christ, who would that person be? If we had a chance to spend fifteen minutes in heaven, how would we spend that time?

Yes, these are random questions, but they make us think about what our life priorities should be. So maybe we should take some time out of our busy days and adjust our priorities, spiritual habits, and use of time by at least making a small attempt at answering these questions. Another random but very pleasant thought is that we're in God's thoughts, according to the Word; that truth puts a big grin all over my face.

Psalm 139:17 says, "How precious to me are your thoughts O God! How vast is the sum of them!"

Small Stuff

The Word tells us to cast all our cares on Him—not just the big stuff, not just the stuff that will matter for eternity, but all our concerns. So we can safely say that if something bothers us, it's a concern of His. I'm an independent type, so I don't like to have to depend on others. There's nothing wrong with that; it can be a good trait. But it can also be something that sometimes hinders us from involving God in our lives.

When we feel like we have control of things, we then think we can fix them ourselves. God just wants us to come to the end of ourselves, and then He likes to step in and help us, even in the small stuff. Really, we can't even think about what the size of "small" is; it varies from person to person. How many times have you asked help from the Almighty to find lost keys? That request seems small when you think about it, but the issue is very big when you want to start your car. So a matter's importance is all in the perspective of the one looking on, but I'm glad to let you know that the star maker loves to hear requests for help, even those that aren't earth shaking.

Psalm 55:22 says, "Cast your burden on the Lord, and He shall sustain you. He shall never permit the righteous to be moved."

The Sacred Moments

The Word tells us that even the bad moments in life can work for the good. If we're playing on a team and are a team player, we will work for the same goal. We work together, we're all on the same page for the game plan, and we listen to our coach. That sounds a lot like what we have to if God can use bad things for good and turn them all around. Working with God, we see things from His point of view and look for opportunities or God moments to help others make it through hardships. This would take the spotlight off us and turn all focus on God. It would make being content wherever we are a whole lot easier, if would think that life had no nonsacred moments. After all, we aren't here by accident but for a purpose.

Many times we think of God as a separate part of our lives. Before leaving the house, we pray for Him to help us through the day; then we go about our day, not giving much thought to Him after we said amen. I love it when I have a project to do, and it seems overwhelming to me, yet a friend comes along and help me see it to the end. This makes the project look doable.

The same could happen by bringing Jesus into the mix more often in our lives. I know it helps to have someone with skin on, but according to the Word, if we have the Spirit of God, He is always there. The Word also tells us we have the Godhead dwelling within us, and it states that the Godhead is over all things our Enemy would use against us. We're always in the presence of God, and what we do with that truth is all up to us. Some days we choose to follow Him and are completely open to hear God's voice. On other days we allow secular moments to override any sacred moments. We need to be sensitive to the voice of God and how He chooses to convey His voice.

First Corinthians 3:9 says, "We are God's workers, working together."

Support Group

We have a great support system in the form of the family of God. We need to recognize that we're in a spiritual battle, and the Enemy wants to see us crash and burn. He wants us to be so busy with our own lives that we miss a fellow soldier who is under attack.

One Sunday evening our pastor asked all of us to stand and join hands; we created a big unbroken circle for prayer. That circle put different visuals in my head of what this act represented, one being the picture of a wall set against any blows to our fellow brother or sister. Another is a blanket that covers him or her from the cold realty of a bad diagnosis, death, or anything else devastating enough to bring someone down. A picture of a good cup of coffee or whatever else makes you happy represents that we can have fellowship with someone who understands and will have our backs. So let's lock arms with fellow believers and ward off whatever the Enemy may use to shoot holes in our armor.

Ecclesiastes 4:12 says, "Though one may be overpowered by another, two can withstand him. And a threefold cord is not quickly broken."

Just a Big Toe Syndrome

Sometimes we may think the body of Christ doesn't need our involvement because we aren't that big of a deal. Though the big toe doesn't get much attention, try breaking it and see how your balance works out. The body of Christ needs everyone doing his or her part in forwarding the kingdom of God. Our part doesn't have to be up in front, in the spotlight, or even in the public eye for us to be useful in the body. We don't see the heart in the physical body, but the body wouldn't be able to function without it.

One day I gave a girl on my softball team some pointers about pitching. I was going back behind the catcher when I heard someone yell my name. I turned around, only to catch that pitch with my nose. I remember bending over in pain, my hands grabbing my face; blood went everywhere. Yes, my nose was broken, and yes, it was painful. But I guarantee you that all my body parts came to attention, all given to my nose.

In other words, my hand didn't slap my nose, saying, "I told you so." Instead it gingerly cradled it while I was on my way to find an ice pack. We all need to come to each other's side when someone is spiritually injured in battle; we shouldn't kick that person when he or she is down. Also when we have physically injured ourselves, some other body part has to compensate for the injury. So it is the same concept spiritually, when we fail to use our gifts God created us to do in the body. Others have to fill in the vacancy, making them do more than their share, which usually ends up in burnout. So let's be the best big toe or whatever body part we do best in making the body of Christ function as a well-oiled machine.

First Corinthians 12:18 says, "But now God has set the members, each one of them, in the body just as He pleased."

In the Eye of a Storm

Life is filled with different situations, difficult people, or drama-filled days. We can decide where we will practice living. We can be the reason for the storm, we can keep the storm brewing, or we can live in the eye of the storm. I live in Wichita, Kansas, known as "tornado alley." Though I've taken cover or watched storms many times, I've never been involved in a tornado. But I've read enough about tornadoes to know there's a calm in the middle, called the "eye" of the storm. Just a few feet outside that eye are terrifying winds and destruction.

Tornadoes have many ratings, as do spiritual storms. We can decide to practice living in the calm right in the middle of the storm by being the peaceful ones in a tense or chaotic gathering, or we can carry peace into a tumultuous situation. When this is our habit of living and bigger storms come that really rock our world, then our first response will be to go straight to the center of calm. Go to the One who speaks peace to His child or that storm.

Mark 4:39 says, "Then He arose and rebuked the wind, and said to the sea, 'Peace by still!' And the wind ceased and there was a great calm."

A Servant's Heart

The Word talks a lot about being a servant. But being a servant isn't a position placed on the resumes of most people who seek to climb the ladder of success. The servant was considered the low man on the totem pole. He wasn't one recognized as being very important to whatever household he was assigned to. The ones being waited on would quickly notice whether the servant didn't show up. Jesus is a prime example for us to follow when it comes to being a servant.

One day at school, one of life's servants ministered to me. A child puked on the floor of my classroom, and I had to leave, or I would have been puking right along with him. As I made the long walk to the office to gather courage, rubber gloves, and cleaning supplies, one of the first-grade teachers saw my discomfort and took on the job. A servant's assignment isn't always glamorous; sometimes you'll get your hands dirty, and some assignments stink. But this child of God was glad that someone had taken on the role of a servant that day and ministered to me and a sick child. When we see a need, it's important to think of others, not what discomfort it will bring to us. Yes, I flunked the test that day, but I'm still so thankful someone was willing to take on the role of a servant. Let's look for ways to minister to others today.

Matthew 20:27–28 says, "And whoever desires to be first among you, let him be your slave. Just as the Son of Man did not come to be served, but to serve and to give His life a ransom for many."

Rockin' the Outfit

Have you ever gotten up in the morning and found that your hair did exactly what it was supposed to do? Maybe your outfit matched, and you felt good in it. Your car was clean and tidy, and you had just brewed the best cup of coffee ever. In other words things were going your way. But then the Kansas wind blew your hair, you spilled coffee on your rockin' outfit, a truck kicked up a rock and cracked your windshield, and company trashed your house.

Sometimes mishaps happen in the spiritual world as well. We wake up forgiven, feeling like we could scale a wall and take on a troop. Everyone in our family is saved. We have a great church, ministry, and God. In other words, everything is spiritually right in or world. But then Christians turn into hypocrites, the devil rains all over our spiritual parade, and we experience trials that would try the patience of Job. The Word tells us to rejoice in everything. Granted, this is easier to do when we're rockin' the great outfit, and we're really feeling the Spirit. But the Word still tells us to rejoice when the wind blows our hair and when the forces of evil make a valiant effort to penetrate our armor of God. We should be known for being the ones in the room who will see the silver lining and the bright side of whatever was tossed in our mix.

Philippians 4:4 says, "Rejoice in the Lord always. Again I will say rejoice!"

Anchors Aweigh

The word *anchor* speaks of stability. Sometimes I float on an air mattress in a pool with my eyes closed. When I open my eyes again, I find myself at the other end, not realizing that I had drifted. There isn't much danger in drifting in a pool, but drifting spiritually can cause some serious problems. When we get away from God and don't allow Him to be our anchor, we give into the flesh and let the winds of adversity blow us off course. Or we get angry and blame our "anchor" or shipmates for what's wrong in our lives. A ship in a storm without the anchor thrown down will drift and become lost. Likewise, if we don't make use of our spiritual anchor, we won't have any stability at all.

The anchor keeps us steady in a storm. We become established by getting to know our "anchor," Christ, through His Word. Some people always look for something that works, so they always change churches, try new methods in the Christian walk, look for other styles of preaching or singing in the church, and so forth. Life changes; hence preachers come and go. Music changes, but the Word of God never changes. Stable people seek God, and we always know how they will react in a storm. They are solid in their beliefs and know where their help comes from. They don't look around for something that works; they already know what works. Let's be the stability a changing world is looking for.

Matthew 24:35 says, "Heaven and earth may pass away, but My Word will by no means pass away."

Caught off Guard

One day I was in my backyard, and the pit bull next door decided to jump the fence and come in my yard. I stood in the middle of the yard, yelling, and the next thing I knew, he jumped back over the fence to his side. I guess I scared him as much as he scared me. That dog took me off guard. That's exactly how Satan works when we let our guard down. An action done over and over becomes a habit. So basically what we do as a habit will determine what we will do when taken off guard.

Do I have a habit of seeing the other person's point of view before making a judgment call? Do I make a habit of walking in the Spirit, or do I first try to walk in the flesh? Do I make it a habit to see what's negative in any situation before seeing what's positive? Do I make it a habit of spouting off my opinion or waiting to hear someone else's first? Do I make it a habit to love and show compassion before I judge? Do I make it a habit to ask God for direction before starting out with just my own logic? Do I make it a habit of returning good for evil, or do I, every once in a while, think I have the right to give someone a little of his or her own medicine? Do I make it a habit to apply the Word, or do I just read the Word? Being taken off guard can happen in many ways. But it's at those times that it will be so important that we have made a conscious effort to create habits that will help us combat those times when we're taken off guard.

First Peter 5:8 says, "Be sober, be vigilant; because your adversary the devil walks about like a roaring lion seeking whom he may devour."

Pleasant Surprises

One morning I reached into my pocket, and to my surprise I pulled out a five-dollar bill. It was not only a surprise but a pleasant one. I love it when we experience pleasant surprises along life's way. You go through the checkout counter and show your coupon; and lo and behold, it's double-coupon day. Maybe you stop at the toll booth and find that the person in the car ahead of you paid your toll. Perhaps you asked for coffee at the end of a meal, and the restaurant didn't charge you. These small things can put a smile on your face.

As a teacher I was surprised when a student brought me a Dr. Pepper. All these examples have happened to me except experiencing double-coupon day and having someone pay my toll. But I've paid someone else's toll, and I know how happy that person was when I did that. God uses events and people to give us little surprises, even when our behavior isn't worthy of receiving them. God gives us surprises when He sees fit to commune with His creation. God gives us surprises when He takes care of us and our needs. He also does this when He lets someone know we could use a word of encouragement or prayer. We could call His surprises blessings or gifts to us. We are truly a blessed people.

Second Corinthians 9:15 says, "Thanks be to God for His indescribable gift!"

Workout Journey

When we join the gym and go to work out, we find many people at different places in their journey to lose weight and get in shape. This discovery can discourage or encourage us, depending on how we care to look at it. I could be very discouraged that I'm faithful to work out, yet it doesn't seem to make a difference as far as weight goes. But then I look around and feel a little more encouraged that there are bigger people than I. But then again, when we make the effort to go, even when it would be easier just to stay at home, we find that we feel better after we stay with it.

All those at the gym have the same goal, but they don't all have the same shapes, workouts, or even levels of endurance. Their final goal is to look smoking hot in their gym clothes. Seriously, when all is said and done, all they want is a great shape. Some have reached their goals and are now working to keep that great shape.

We're like that spiritually. All of us are on a journey; we're all at different places on that journey, and some are maturing in the Lord, while others are just starting out. But just like all those at the gym, they all started at the same place on their quest to get into shape. Everyone's spiritual journey starts at the same place, and that's at the cross. I could look at others, see how great they look, and wish I looked like that. Or I could just keep going to the gym and being faithful to my workout. The same is true spiritually. We can't look around and compare ourselves with others, but we must be faithful with what God has shown us, for after all, that is what we will be responsible for.

Second Corinthians 10:12 says, "For we dare not class ourselves or compare ourselves with those who commend themselves. But they measuring themselves by themselves and comparing themselves among themselves are not wise."

No More Sin

Someday there will be no sin. We can't imagine a world where there is no sin, because that is all we've known here on earth. We look around us and think this world is going downhill—and fast. That assumption is correct. But whenever we complain that we dislike our life or our lot in life, we can trace it all back to sin. With all our failures, we can go back to the fact that they were rooted in sin. So basically, if humans are still here, there is sin with all kinds of labels attached. But one day it will be enough, and Satan and his entourage of demons will be bound and thrown into the place created just for him and his fallen cohorts.

With sin erased, there will be no need for prayer for a body waging a war with cancer, no more sickness of any kind, no more broken hearts, no more broken promises, no more phone calls letting us know of any more bad news, and no more crying over things we have no control over. If it's bad in any shape or form, it will come to an end. We have the hope that sin won't win. Let's encourage ourselves in the Lord and remind each other that the great day of the Lord will soon be here.

Revelation 20:1–2 says, "Then I saw an angel coming down from heaven, having the key to the bottomless pit and a great chain in his hand. He laid hold of the dragon, that serpent of old who is the Devil, and bound him for a thousand years."

Steadfast or Stubborn

We can be steadfast without being stubborn. Sometimes we think we're being consistent and not compromising our beliefs or giving in to every wind that blows, when really all we're doing at times is being stubborn. There is a fine line between being steady and being stubborn. We have to think about what our motives really are behind our decisions to not move or our reasons for not budging on something. Just because something has always been this way doesn't mean something new won't work. The older we get, the more steadfast we can become in our own way of doing life. Sometimes we must be open to something we may not have done before, especially if it works a whole lot better. We know we're maturing in the Lord when in getting older we can still make changes that will make us a better person. Should we be steadfast in our walk? Oh yes, but not stubbornly so.

First Corinthians 15:58 says, "Therefore my beloved brethren be steadfast, immovable, always abounding in the work of the Lord, knowing that your labor is not in vain in the Lord."

I'm a Survivor

One Saturday I attended a women's conference in Missouri, and the speaker asked us, "Who has survived?" Everyone immediately thought the speaker was talking about breast cancer, since she was a cancer survivor, so only a few people stood to their feet. But she responded that she hadn't said, "Have you survived cancer?" She'd just asked, "Who has survived?"

Even if we aren't at the end of whatever valley we're walking through, even if we're standing tall, still hanging on to Jesus and trusting in Him for the outcome, we're among the survivors. Some issues will be ongoing, but if we're depending on God's help, then we're among survivors. We can share our stories of survival, whatever those may be, with others so they can use the encouragement of the survivor story to help them in their season of walking through the valley.

When I moved into a house I had purchased, I discovered that the former owner had planted rose bushes everywhere in the backyard. Well, due to my lack of gardening abilities, they grew out of control. Even when I didn't take good care of them and chopped them to the ground, guess what they did the next year? You guessed it; they bloomed again. So no matter what the Enemy does to cut us down, usually using circumstances or even people, we can come back just as strong or even stronger than before.

Romans 5:3–4 says, "And not only that, but we also glory in tribulations, knowing that tribulation produces perseverance, and perseverance, character; and character hope."

Passing with Flying Colors

"You passed with flying colors" are great words to receive for whatever occasion they are connected to. A kid loves to hear a teacher say those words. A patient loves hearing them from his or her doctor. The teen driver loves to hear them from the DMV. For any person waiting on results of any kind, those words are music to his or her ears. A test is intended to reveal whether we're retaining, learning, or developing in whatever area we're being tested in.

What a great feeling of fulfillment we have when we can go to the next level, receive that promotion, or just know we've cleared another hurdle. God gives us tests to see whether we're going to choose to walk in the Spirit or the flesh. Let's not just pass but pass with flying colors. Life is full of tests of all sizes. What's important isn't about the size of the test but about our passing the test. Will we flunk a test every now and again? Oh my word, you better believe it! But how sweet it is when we pass tests with the help of the Holy Spirit working in and through us.

First Peter 1:7 says, "That the genuineness of your faith, being much more precious than gold that perishes though it is tested by fire, may be found to praise, honor, and glory at the revelation of Jesus Christ."

Walk in Truth

In a world filled with chronic liars, deceitfulness, and truth twisters, it's nice to know we don't have to lie our way through life. By walking in the truth set for us in the Bible, we can more easily not fall prey to saying something that isn't the truth or twisting the truth to fit our story.

Lying is a habit with so many people today. Some people wouldn't know the truth if it slapped them up the side of the head. The truth can be stretched to make the story more entertaining, it can be twisted to help cover our tails, or it can be bent to help move our agendas. Lying can be done without even batting an eye. God calls lying a sin; man calls it a bad habit or mistake. God expects us to repent when it happens; man just says to deal with it and moves on. For those of us who don't make lying a habit, walking in the truth can mean that we make a point of walking in what light and truth have been revealed to us on or pathway. But if I ask you whether I look fat, go right ahead, lie to me, and say I look great! God will completely understand! Seriously, we need to make a point to walk in the light of God's Word today. If we do, we will have a leg up on those who want to twist the Scripture and try to lead us astray.

Proverbs 14:5 says, "A faithful witness does not lie. But a false witness will utter lies."

Lesson Learned from a Jigsaw Puzzle

I've never enjoyed putting puzzles together. For one reason, I don't have the patience to put all the same-colored pieces together, put all the corner pieces together in a pile, or just turn all the pieces on the same side. I just want to get started already, but there are five thousand pieces to the puzzle; so after looking at the pile before me, I'm ready to just forget it. The picture on the outside of the box looks cool, but to get there seems a little impossible.

I have a friend who can do puzzles with ease. I want to force the pieces to fit, because they look like the same shape and color, so why don't they want to fit? That brings us to wanting to put the puzzle pieces of life together without having the patience to pray or wait on God. We may have made impulsive decisions or just relied on our own understanding of things that made our life puzzle seem forced to fit or work out. I liked to mess with my friend, and I would just put pieces together where obviously they didn't go. My friend just shook her head and calmly put the pieces where they were meant to be.

We see the same response from God when we try hard to make our plans, wishes, or even our prayers fit into our preconceived idea of what should be the outcome of whatever we're asking God to do in our life puzzle. Isaiah instructs us to wait on the Lord. We may need more patience to wait for answers but keep the desire to allow God to be the One to put each piece of our life puzzle in place. I know a puzzle can be a work of art when finished, because I have a beautiful puzzle framed and hanging on my living room wall; it all started in a box. God can make our lives masterpieces if we completely leave the placement of puzzle pieces up to Him.

Proverbs 3:5–6 says, "Trust in the Lord with all your heart and lean not on your own understanding. In your ways acknowledge Him and He shall direct your paths."

Doughnut Holes

I love doughnuts and doughnut holes, but I dislike burning off the calories and pounds they add to my middle. But this mentality of being undisciplined is what we see more and more of in society and even in the church. We want life to be easy; we want something, but we don't want to do the work to get it, and we don't want to be told what to do through any of it.

As a teacher, I see this mentality in kids who come through my classroom. Many kids don't know how to do things on their own; they can't think for themselves, and they want more and more things instead of being grateful for what they have. They tend to be lazy and very touchy when it comes to discipline or correction. But this tendency can also describe the church as well. We want everything at our fingertips; hence we don't have a complete trust in God to meet our needs. We do just enough to get by spiritually and really aren't zealous or see the need to do more than is necessary for God; we lack passion in our walk with Christ.

Since we aren't committed, we become very touchy when someone criticizes or corrects us. So when we take in more than we give out and keep sitting on a pew, getting fed and not sharing that Word, it's like me sitting at the table, eating doughnuts, and not doing something to burn off those calories. We become overweight saints of God; someone might be hungry for what we received from the table, but we don't bother to share it with them. Kids are more and more satisfied with just what's average or mediocre, and nothing is extraordinary.

We have an awesome God who is just waiting for His kids to do something or to be someone out of the ordinary with His help. So let's do that with all our hearts, souls, and bodies—and do so with gusto.

Colossians 3:23 says, "And whatever you do, do it heartily as to the Lord and not to men."

Watch That Tone

Our tone can speak volumes in describing how we're feeling. Our tone can let people know we're frustrated, mad, or happy. Our tones can come across sarcastically or just downright hatefully. One day I came across harshly and sarcastically. In my head I didn't sound harsh, but I was. The way I knew for sure was the look that came across the student's face after I said what I did. Therefore, I wasn't convicted of what I had said but how I had said it. I immediately apologized to the student and felt much better after doing so, and I received a great response from the child.

When we're checked by the Holy Spirit about something, we need to correct it right then. We shouldn't continue doing the wrong deed for the rest of the day, making excuses for our behavior and then having a bad day to boot. So just as it's great to feel the Spirit of God on Sunday, it's good to have the conviction of God on Monday. Though I liked the feeling on Sunday much more than I did on Monday, I'm truly thankful that I felt the conviction of the Spirit. We need to have a tender heart, in which the Spirit of God feels most at home.

Proverbs 15:23 says, "A man has joy by the answer of his mouth. And a word spoken in due season, how good it is!"

Touchy-Feely Kind

One weekend I ran into two different situations that made me realize something about touch. I have a friend who is a germophobe; therefore, the least amount of touching she does, the better she likes it. I also talked to a guy who'd recently had a stroke. His sense of touch had been greatly affected. He told me he could feel only a little bit after being paralyzed.

Really, even if we say we aren't the touchy-feely type, we're created to respond to touch. The germophobe will touch those he or she loves without getting out the disinfectant, and the guy who had the stroke works hard during therapy to get his sense of touch back. So, in other words, we're built for touch.

If we were to read the Word, we would see that Jesus's ministry was filled with not only teaching but also touching. He reached out and touched people when He healed them. He touched those whom others avoided altogether. The Word speaks of a woman who just needed to touch His garment.

Sometimes words aren't needed when you can place our hands on someone's shoulder, caress a face, or hug someone to say, "I'm sorry," "I love you," or "I care about what you're facing." Today society has made touching a bad, dirty, or downright abusive thing. Our words can mean nothing when we don't want to be involved enough at the right time to offer our sense of touch. We can be so concerned about people being in our bubble or space that we completely miss seeing that we had an opportunity to reach out and touch someone's life. Don't be discouraged if you're one of those people who aren't touchy-feely types; there's still hope for us to learn this lesson.

Matthew 9:21 says, "For she said to herself, 'If only I may touch His garment. I shall be made well.'"

Wishing Our Lives Away

I know as a teacher that I've been guilty of counting down days to summer break. Then after school starts, the countdown begins all over again as I count the days until the first long weekend, Thanksgiving break, Christmas break, spring break, and any birthday the school lets us take off. And before I know it, I've wished away another school year. Here's an idea. Let's live each day with the same intensity as if we're looking forward to the next break away from work. After all, vacations finally arrive, and they are soon over.

The Word talks about kingdom living, which is here and now. We prepare ourselves for eternity, which is in the future, but live it right now. So it's easy for people to look down the road to when they will retire, get married, or be promoted. All these events are good, but we forget to relax and put ourselves more into the present moments leading up to those times that are in our futures.

We've all been guilty of saying on one day or another, "Will this day never end?" Yes, it will, but what good did we accomplish, or how did we show others that we knew Christ? Not to be a downer, but retirement may never come. Getting married or getting that promotion may not be in the cards for our lives. But what we did with day-to-day moments will be what will live on and be remembered after we're gone. Don't wish it all away by counting down to the next planned or exciting moment.

Ecclesiastes 3:1 says, "To everything there is a season. A time for every purpose under heaven."

Finding God's Will

People waste a lot of time trying to search for or figure out what they think God's will for their life is. God will open or close doors; all the while we're already doing what we know is right. That will happen on a daily basis. We're given opportunities to do something for God when we're busy doing our best at what we do best. We already know God doesn't give our lives purpose via audio, visions, or bubble letters in the sky. He lets us know when we follow what is already given to us in His Word. Sometimes we want to be what we want to be *right now*, just jumping in without doing the work that goes along with it. We do the same thing in God's work. But He will use those who are faithful in doing what could be mundane yet needed tasks of this thing called life. When we move with God, not ahead of God, we can sit back and watch Him work and see His hand in our lives.

Hebrews 13:21 says, "Make you complete in every good work to do His will, working in you what is well pleasing in His sight, through Jesus Christ to whom be glory forever and ever. Amen."

Are You Packing Heat?

Today we hear a lot about conceal and carry, and getting the license to carry a gun. I don't care for guns, so I still have yet to get my conceal and carry permit. I've chosen to hang out with my friends who have this right. So when we think of weapons in today's world, our minds immediately go to a gun.

But the Enemy of our souls will use more subtle means to shoot us down spiritually. He uses surprise attacks and blindside us when we leave our guards down. Other weapons he uses are our negative and degrading words, our ugly and dark moods, or our knee-jerk reactions with little or no thought. The biggest one is just doing nothing. No progress is made spiritually when these weapons are being used. But we can take these weapons out of his hands when we use our sword or the Word to rebuke him, our helmet to guard our minds against negative or wrong thoughts, or the breastplate to ward off blows to our heart, which contains our emotions and will. But just as a seat belt in a car is useless unless it's buckled, air bags are useless unless they are deployed. Just as a bulletproof vest is useless unless it's worn, so doing nothing spiritually is useless when warding off the advances to our souls. We can't just say we own the equipment to fight against those weapons brought against us; we have to enter each day wearing the equipment. What does that look like? We think before we speak or act, we forgive, we love, we serve, and we refuse to be shaken by others through their negative words, bad attitudes, or hateful actions. So go ahead. Pack the heat. But don't forget your sword!

Hebrews 4:12 says, "For the word of God is living and powerful, and sharper than any two-edged sword, piercing even to the division of soul and spirit, and of joints and marrow, and is a discerner of the thoughts and intents of the heart."

Not One of My Best Days

Have you ever had days that don't make the list of your "top five days of all time"? I have, and it hasn't been so long ago. I really needed to be a better example of a forgiven child of God. Did I kill someone? No. Did I steal something? No. Did I lie? No. But if we claim to be forgiven children of God, we need to act like we are. After all, we're made in God's image and were adopted into His family, so we need to show some resemblance to our older brother, Jesus.

In other words, when I asked whether I had killed someone (though I might have felt like it), the answer was a big no. But we kill our testimony when we don't show God's traits or the fruit of the Spirit. When I asked whether I had stolen anything, I gave another no answer. But I allowed the devil to steal from me the benefits of walking in the Spirit. When I asked whether I had lied, I didn't do so on purpose. But I lied when I said I was fine or just peachy when really I could have used a big dose of Jesus. It's when we have those kinds of days that it's very reassuring when we can read in Hebrews 13:8 that God is the same all the time; we may change, but God never does. He doesn't change, but His creation does. So it's also reassuring in that same book in the Bible that we have a High Priest we can go to when we make a mess of our day.

Hebrews 4:16 says, "Let us therefore come boldly to the throne of grace, that we may obtain mercy and find grace to help in time of need."

What to Put On

Every night when I'm getting ready for the next day, I have to decide what in the world I'm going to wear. We're concerned about what we will use to cover our physical bodies, but in the Word, God tells us what to put on spiritually. He tells us to be kind, humble, gentle, and patient—and to wear those characteristics every day. Sometimes that is a hard outfit to model. But it's possible, or He wouldn't have told us to do it.

It will probably be easy to grab the humble shirt but harder to match it with the pair of patient pants. Sometimes the kind socks are mismatched with a not-too-kind attitude. Or the gentle pair of shoes may pinch our feet when we want to lose our gentleness and come across harshly. But just as we can make the comfortable choice of an outfit we feel good about wearing physically, so can we make a conscious decision to spiritually put on what God wants to be identified as one of His own. So go look in the mirror and tell your reflection that you're looking good, but don't fail to look in the mirror of God's Word and make sure your reflection has Jesus all over it.

Colossians 3:12 says, "Therefore as the elect of God holy and beloved, put on tender mercies, kindness, humility, meekness, longsuffering."

Vulnerable

No one wants to admit that he or she is vulnerable. That sounds like we're weak or that we don't have control over something. But really everyone has a spot that is vulnerable. It may be with a relationship or a situation that keeps showing up in our lives. It doesn't matter whether we have Christ; we're subject to vulnerability. The feeling is best described as being in someone's crosshairs; we're just standing in the open with no protection or ammunition. We have no idea where the shooter is located until we're hit, and then the wound is open again.

What I just described would be us being vulnerable in our physically beings. But we're also vulnerable in our spiritual lives. No one is exempt. If we think we are, then we're sadly mistaken. If we aren't going to admit to it, then the Enemy will see to it that he finds our spiritually vulnerable spot, and no one wants that to happen. So blessed is the person who recognizes his or her weak spots and takes action for protection before Satan attacks.

Since we're human, our feelings can be hurt in our emotional or physical being; but it's so awesome that we don't have to be open to the spiritual attacks of the devil, because we have Someone who has our back and will see the shooter before he take us out. It's also awesome if we physically feel vulnerable with a situation or person; we have friends and family who will look out for us as well.

Second Timothy 2:26 says, "And that they may come to their senses and escape the snare of the devil, having been taken captive by him to do his will."

Worship

We're sometimes so concerned about the way we worship that we forget who we're worshipping. Think about what divides churches many times. Isn't it disagreements over methods of worship?

The book of Psalms gives us the guide for praise. Sometimes we don't even know what to pray or how to pray. We may be so low that we can't speak, let alone pray. But the Word tells us that God knows our hearts. At times I feel, in corporate worship times, that I'm being told how to worship. "Raise your hand, stand up, come forward." I'm not saying any of those things are bad, but worship is between us and our God. Spontaneity in worship is what I love, the kind of worship that rises up inside. You let it come out by shedding tears, raising your hands, standing up, shouting a praise, or just sitting quietly in His presence.

The psalmist wrote his worship songs out of bitterness, sadness, discouragement, and sinfulness, but he always ending up showing his praise to his Redeemer and giving Him thanks. At the end of the day, the child of God knows God deserves our praise and worship. The bottom line is that God wants our worship, but He wants it to come from an honest heart that is transparent before Him.

Psalm 147:1 says, "Praise the Lord! For it is good to sing praises to our God. For it is pleasant, and praise is beautiful."

The Last Chapter

We win! I read the last chapter of the book, and Revelation is all about who is going to overcome and who will have the final say. But the Word also warns us about the last days and what to watch for. There will be false teachers peddling false doctrine. As it says in Ephesians 6:12; we don't fight against flesh and blood but against spirits. But be encouraged; we have someone inside us who is bigger than anyone in the world. He has defeated the evil spirit invading our culture and society, so we don't have to succumb to what society dishes out as politically correct or just people's rights. The Enemy would have us to fear, to duck our tails, and to run. But we aren't just survivors; we're overcomers. The news may look bleak, the economy may have gone south, and our society may have taken on a godless belief system. But heads up, faithful pilgrim. We aren't home yet. We can rest in the fact that the One we're following home has this one, and we win.

First John 4:4 says, "You are of God, little children, and have overcome them, because He who is in you is greater than he who is in the world."

Printed in the United States
By Bookmasters